射撃塔

逆探

―― 15m測距儀
―― 防空指揮所
―― 第1艦橋
―― 2.5m測距儀
―― 第2艦橋　IV－13㎜M.G.
―― 8m測距儀
司令塔　　1番副砲塔　III－15.5㎝砲　　2番主砲塔
　　　　　　　　　15m測距儀
　　　　　　　　　　　　III－46㎝砲　　　　　　　　　　　　　　　　　　　25㎜M.G.
　　　　　　　　　　　　15m測距儀
　　　　　　　　　　　　1番主砲塔　III－46㎝砲

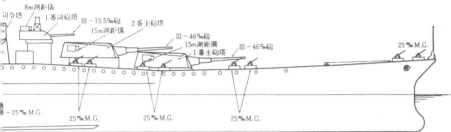

―25㎜M.G.
　　　　25㎜M.G.　　　25㎜M.G.　　　25㎜M.G.

5㎜M.G.　　25㎜M.G.
　　　　　　　　　　　　25㎜M.G.
　　　　　　　　　　　　　　　　25㎜M.G.
　　　　　　　　　　　　　　　　　　　　25㎜M.G.

15.5㎝砲　　46㎝砲　　46㎝砲

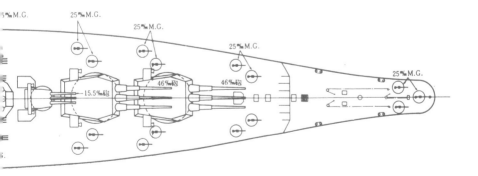

0　　　10　　　20　　　30　　　40　　　50m

# BATTLESHIP MUSASHI

# BATTLESHIP MUSASHI

## The Making and Sinking of the World's Biggest Battleship

Akira Yoshimura

Translated by
Vincent Murphy

KODANSHA INTERNATIONAL
Tokyo • New York • London

Originally published by Shinchosha, Ltd., under the title *Senkan Musashi*.

Previously published as *Build the Musashi: The Birth and Death of the World's Greatest Battleship.*

Distributed in the United States by Kodansha America, Inc., 575 Lexington Avenue, New York N.Y. 10022, and in the United Kingdom and continental Europe by Kodansha Europe Ltd., 95 Aldwych, London WC2B 4JF. Published by Kodansha International Ltd., 17-14 Otowa 1-chome, Bunkyo-ku, Tokyo 112-8652, and Kodansha America, Inc.

Hardcover edition, 1991
Paperback edition, 1999
99 00 01 02 10 9 8 7 6 5 4 3 2 1
ISBN 4-7700-2400-2

# Contents

# Prologue

The Musashi *was in trouble. It had managed to outmaneuver several torpedoes, but one of the deadly fish had gotten through, ripping into its hull on the starboard bow and destroying its sounding room. Clouds of toxic gas filled the forward infirmary, suffocating the wounded.*

*Minutes later another formation of enemy planes appeared on the horizon. They closed in fast, dropping their torpedoes from a great height. The weapons fell spiraling into the sea, carving the water's surface with a great net of crisscrossing trails. Most headed for the* Musashi.

*"Full turn to starboard! Reverse direction hard aport!" The chief navigator screamed frantically over the main deck speakers.*

*The ship lurched violently as three more torpedoes found their mark, two to port, one to starboard. Torrential waves from the explosions crashed over the main deck, sweeping a tide of blood and dismembered bodies before them.*

*"Can still travel at twenty-four knots," the* Musashi *signaled to the* Yamato *after the attack.*

*The fleet held its formation. The* Musashi *zigzagged in wide sweeps along with the rest of the ships of the First Squadron. One-third of its machine gunners were dead or wounded, but the rest continued to concentrate fire overhead. Enemy aircraft dropped into the sea, but the Americans were relentless. The next attack struck the port and starboard sides, followed immediately by two more torpedoes to starboard. Seawater poured into the vessel's*

7

*lower decks. Then a bomb made a direct hit in the bow area of the main deck, killing scores of doctors and wounded crewmen in the forward infirmary.*

*Torpedo damage was concentrated in the Musashi's mid to fore sections, and the entire area under the fore section's mid-deck was flooded. The bow was at a ten degree list to starboard. The defense director activated the ship's pumping system and took measures to prevent further flooding.*

*"Twenty-two knots possible," the Musashi reported, its speed only slightly hampered by the damage. It continued zigzagging along with the fleet. The enemy aircraft had gone.*

*"Gunners may leave their stations," sounded over the speakers, and the exhausted men dropped to their knees. The main deck was littered with gore, and the screaming of the wounded cut through the silence like a jagged blade.*

*The air ducts and hatches to the main deck had been shut during the attack. Hot exhaust fumes from the engines filled the ship's hull, making the heat on the lower decks almost unbearable. The able-bodied burst topside into the open air drenched in sweat.*

*The forward infirmary, where the surviving injured sat silently in shock, was awash with blood. The functioning areas of the ship's infirmaries could not handle the unrelenting flow of injured, and casualties overflowed into the nearby officers' quarters.*

*The Musashi's damage control crew was unable to correct the battleship's forward list. A torpedo, entering through an opening made by a previous explosion, had penetrated the ship's underwater defenses. The list in the bow reduced the vessel's speed to sixteen knots, and it soon fell far behind the rest of the fleet.*

*The enemy realized that the loss of the Musashi would be a serious blow to the Japanese Navy, and the attack planes had concentrated their firepower on her alone, leaving the other vessels virtually unscathed. Now, like a great but mortally wounded beast, it struggled, trailing the fleet as it slowly disappeared over the horizon.*

# 1
# Boom to Bust and Back

1857–1933

The Nagasaki Shipyard was established in 1857 by the shogunal government as the first shipyard in Japan to build western-style ships. In 1885 the Meiji government sold the yard to Yataro Iwasaki, the founder of Mitsubishi, still one of Japan's largest industrial conglomerates.

During the Meiji (1868–1912) and Taisho (1912–1926) periods, the shipyard produced first-class commercial vessels such as the *Tatsuta-maru* and the *Asama-maru*, as well as large-scale warships such as the 31,260-ton battleship *Hyuga*, the 39,900-ton battleship *Tosa*, and the 27,500-ton battle cruiser *Kirishima*. The Nagasaki Shipyard was one of the few shipbuilding facilities in Japan producing all types of naval vessels, including the first-line cruisers *Furutaka*, *Aoba*, *Haguro*, *Chokai*, *Mikuma*, *Tone*, and *Chikuma*, which saw action during the Pacific War.

In the decades preceding World War One, the yard was heavily subsidized by the government and grew in tempo with Japan's rapid capitalist expansion. At its peak in the early 1920s the shipyard reached a total area of twenty-five acres, with a shipbuilding area of thirteen acres and a work force of over 15,000. Before reaching this enormous size, however, the shipyard went through a violent series of economic ups and downs, especially during the ten-year period following the end of the Taisho period.

After World War One the Japanese shipbuilding industry was in the midst of an unprecedented boom. Full order books for commercial vessels were boosted by a naval shipbuilding program that the

Japanese Navy announced after the U.S. Navy obtained Congress's approval to add ten new battleships and six new battle cruisers to its fleet in 1916.

With the onset of a naval arms race between Japan and the United States, the U.S. Navy proposed a second large-scale expansion plan of its battleship fleet. This also elicited a response from the Japanese Navy, which managed to push a proposal for naval construction through the Imperial Diet in 1920. The program called for the building of 192 vessels, including cruisers, destroyers, and submarines, as well as battle cruisers and battleships.

The competition for naval supremacy between Japan and the United States ran contrary to international efforts to maintain peace in the early 1920s. The interwar years were a period of economic instability in the U.S. and Europe, and Western governments found it increasingly difficult to bear the burden of military expansion.

At this time of restraint in the West, Japan was in an even greater state of social and economic bankruptcy. The economy slid from the boom years of World War One to an economic downturn in 1920, with demonstrations by both farmers and workers. Facing a national economic crisis, Japan was forced to conform to the world trend toward disarmament and took part in the Washington Conference in 1921. The following year Japan signed the Washington Treaty, which limited the size, armament, and deployment of the capital ships of the United States, Britain, and Japan at a ratio of five-five-three.

With this treaty, the Japanese Navy's proposal for an eight-eight fleet (eight battleship-eight cruiser) was no longer feasible. The only capital ships that the Japanese Navy was allowed to retain were six battleships: the *Mutsu*, the *Yamato*, the *Fuso*, the *Yamashiro*, the *Ise*, and the *Hyuga*; and four battle cruisers: the *Kongo*, the *Hiei*, the *Haruna*, and the *Kirishima*. Naval vessels that were under construction at the time were scrapped and dismantled.

The shipbuilding industry, already suffering from the postwar economic depression, was crippled by the cancellation of naval contracts. After initial lay-offs involving thousands of workers at naval arsenals, civilian shipyards also began reducing their work forces, sparking off widespread industrial unrest.

The Nagasaki Shipyard was building the battleship *Tosa* and the battle cruiser *Takao* as part of the eight-eight fleet plan when the Washington Treaty was signed. The government ordered the Navy to scrap the *Tosa*, after the incomplete hull had been launched. Construction work was also halted on the *Takao*.

After the orders for the *Tosa*'s destruction came through, 50,000 shipyard workers and Nagasaki citizens watched it being towed out to sea by five tugboats. The incomplete hull was first taken to the Kure Arsenal, where it was battered at the arsenal's torpedo test range, and then towed to the Seto Inland Sea, where it was shot at and bombed at the Kamegakubi test range. The test firing began in June 1924, and within only a few months the *Tosa* was a bullet-torn hunk of steel. The hull was disposed of like all other Navy scrap metal, in the Tosa Gulf—its namesake in Japan's Pacific waters.

The workers of the Nagasaki Shipyard mourned the destruction of the ship they had invested so much time in, but the executives of the yard were more in shock than mourning. First there was the large financial loss the shipyard had sustained from the cancellation on the *Tosa* and the *Takao*. Five years later came the worldwide panic triggered by the Great Depression of 1929. On top of that, the limitation on the construction of naval support ships and a five-year extension of the Washington Treaty, which was agreed at the London Naval Disarmament Conference of 1930, brought the Nagasaki Shipyard to the verge of bankruptcy.

Mitsubishi followed the example of other shipyards in Japan by closing plants and progressively laying off thousands of employees. Within two years the number of workers at the Nagasaki Shipyard shrank to one-third the number employed during the construction of the *Tosa*.

The shipbuilding industry finally began showing signs of recovery at about the time of the Manchurian Incident (1931). A group

11

of high-ranking Navy officers, known as the "fleet faction," were expressing dissatisfaction with the five-five-three ratio. As the faction gathered supporters in the government, it seemed increasingly likely that Japan would break the Washington Treaty.

In 1933 Foreign Minister Yosuke Matsuoka announced Japan's withdrawal from the League of Nations, when the league-sponsored Lytton Commission condemned Japan's invasion of Manchuria. With the worsening of Japan's relations with the U.S. and Britain, the executives at the Nagasaki Shipyard saw little likelihood of the treaty limiting naval construction being extended beyond its expiration date of 1935.

As soon as the Navy decided to break the treaty, the naval arms race between the United States and Japan would begin again. It was also safe to assume that the new ships would be even larger than the 40,000-ton *Tosa*, which had been commissioned for the eight-eight fleet plan.

# 2

# The Oath of Secrecy

**Summer 1937**

In late June 1937 a group of engineers, led by Kumao Baba, disappeared from their posts at the Nagasaki Shipyard. Since he was one of the senior members of the Engineering Department's Shipbuilding Division, Baba's absence was especially noticeable.

In February of that year Baba had received instructions from Kensuke Watanabe, director of the shipyard's steel mill, to prepare a large number of wooden blocks by the following April for the construction of an important vessel. The cedar blocks were to be made into the model forms that would be used in the process of measuring and manufacturing the actual deck plates for the ship.

Baba was astonished by the number of blocks Watanabe had ordered. "Do you need that many for only one ship?" he asked.

Watanabe shot him a hard, imperious look and snapped at him to gather the blocks without further questions. Baba was stunned; he had never seen the director so short-tempered and impatient.

After having the blocks prepared, Baba was again approached by Watanabe, who, with the same terse manner, ordered the engineer to follow him to the office of the shipyard's president. Entering the office behind Watanabe, Baba found himself before a group of shipyard executives and Navy officers sitting around a large conference table.

Attending the meeting were Captain Shuji Hirata, the chief supervisor of naval construction, a Navy officer attached to a civilian shipyard, President Kyosuke Tamai, and engineers Masanao Serikawa and Shigeichi Koga. The importance of the meeting was

13

immediately apparent to Baba, who half hid behind Watanabe's corpulent form.

After Baba and Watanabe had taken their seats, Captain Hirata addressed the group.

"As everyone here—with the exception of Baba—knows, the Nagasaki Shipyard has been chosen to construct a new battleship. This project has been classified top secret, and we have been ordered to assign only absolutely trustworthy employees to it. Each of you has been checked out by the secret police. Your political and religious beliefs, family backgrounds, and contacts with foreigners have proven to be acceptable for the project. However, in order to further assure absolute confidentiality from all of you, we would like you to swear an oath of secrecy."

The captain then took a piece of paper out of a drawer. The document was passed around the table until it finally reached Baba, who glanced over it quickly.

### OATH OF SECRECY

I am aware that all work involving the construction of the No. 2 Battleship is vital to national security. I will make the utmost effort to maintain the secrecy of the project, and swear that I will leak no information relating to the said battleship, even to relatives and close friends. In the event that I should violate this oath, I will submit to the punishment determined by the company and the Navy.

Mitsubishi Heavy Industries Co., Inc., Nagasaki Shipyard
Name:              Seal:              Occupation:
Date:         / /1937

Baba was taken aback by all this ceremony, but he followed Watanabe, Serikawa, and Koga in signing and placing his personal seal on the oath.

Captain Hirata continued, "I would like you all to keep this oath foremost in your minds as you work on the No. 2 Battleship project. From now on, you are all considered temporary members of the Navy. The president of the plant will be treated as an honorary vice admiral, and the engineers as officers."

When the meeting ended Baba and the other engineers left the office, while Tamai and Hirata remained behind.

Baba caught up with Watanabe and asked in a low voice, "What do you know about this No. 2 Battleship they were talking about?"

"Nothing!" Watanabe snapped nervously. "Don't talk about it! Don't even tell anyone you took an oath."

The director looked frightened, and Baba backed away.

Before he had even been able to gather his thoughts, Baba had been informed that the secret police had completely investigated his background. Then he had been ordered to sign an oath of secrecy. He wondered what was meant by the sentence "I will submit to the punishment decided by the company and the Navy."

* * *

It rained almost continuously that June. Baba, wearing an old rubber raincoat, was supervising some outside work one afternoon when he received a summons from Watanabe. Baba put another man in charge of his team and quickly trudged through the rain to the director's office.

"Take ten blueprinters with you to the Kure Naval Arsenal," Watanabe ordered. "They have begun preparations for the construction of the No. 1 Battleship. Our No. 2 Battleship will be built to the same specifications. We want you to copy the measurements from the No. 1 Battleship for our reference here."

After this brief explanation Watanabe told Baba he was to leave on June 23. Baba was in the middle of supervising the finishing touches on a 6,702-ton passenger ship for the Takachiho Steamship Company. When Baba pointed out that his deadline for the project was the end of June, Watanabe simply told him to find someone else to finish the project.

"Just don't tell anyone you're going to Kure," he said.

Baba nodded, wondering how he would arrange a trip to Kure at such short notice.

Later that afternoon, ten assistant engineers filed into Watanabe's office. They, too, had taken an oath of secrecy some days before.

Watanabe began by warning them about maintaining the confidentiality of the project. "As you were all told by the chief supervisor, the construction of the No. 2 Battleship is a top military secret, and we don't want anyone inside or outside the plant to know that you're going to Kure. Keep it secret!"

He divided the men into two groups, the first to set off for Kure during the day, and the second the same evening. On the day of his departure Baba explained to his family that he would have to make a short business trip. He slung a small travel bag over his shoulder and slipped quietly out of his family home and down the long alleyways to Nagasaki Station. Baba recognized one of his subordinates at the station but ignored him, deliberately boarding a different car, so as not to draw attention to the fact they were leaving on the same train.

In Kure, Baba avoided the hotel where he usually stayed on his business trips, taking a room at the small inn where the other engineers were spending the night. Before leaving Nagasaki the eleven-man team had agreed to stay in separate rooms and not to communicate while in the inn as a security precaution. They passed one another in the corridors that night but did not even exchange greetings.

The next morning, after each member of the group had left the hotel separately, the engineers gathered at the front gate of the Kure Naval Arsenal. Watanabe, who had left Nagasaki the night before, showed up at 9 A.M. The engineers were thoroughly searched at the arsenal gates. Once inside the compound, they followed Watanabe to the office of the arsenal's director of naval construction, Rear Admiral Shigeharu Kuwabara.

Watanabe introduced his team to the admiral and assured him that each man had been fingerprinted and photographed. After making the arrangements for the team's stay, Watanabe said his farewells and left the office with Baba.

"I expect you to do a good job," Watanabe said, as they walked briskly toward the arsenal gates. "I'm counting on you."

Baba's first task was to take his team to the dry dock where the hull of the No. 1 Battleship was being built under the supervision of thirty-eight-year-old Commander Masao Kajiwara.

Kajiwara immediately called the project's head blueprinter, whom Baba recognized as Kageo Tsuji, an engineer who had previously worked at the Mitsubishi Shipyard in Nagasaki. Tsuji was a naval engineer who had risen through the ranks after graduating from the Naval Engineering Academy. In contrast to many other men in his position of authority, Tsuji was known for his kindness and common sense. Baba and Tsuji greeted one another like old friends, and the blueprinter sat down to explain his responsibilities on the battleship project.

The No. 2 Battleship to be built in Nagasaki would have identical specifications to the No. 1 Battleship now under construction in Kure. The basic blueprints for the No. 1 Battleship had been given to the Kure Arsenal by the Bureau of Naval Construction and had been copied by Lieutenant Commander Shigeru Makino, who was the head of design for the No. 1 Battleship. Makino's blueprints were then handed over to the engineers in charge of building the hull.

Using these partial blueprints, Baba would be able to prepare the forms that he needed to begin construction on Nagasaki's No. 2 Battleship. A single set of forms would be submitted to the arsenal's steel mill to make the decks for both battleships. It was Baba's responsibility to supervise the making of the forms, and to arrange to send the deck of the No. 2 Battleship to Nagasaki after it was manufactured in Kure.

Baba and his team of engineers started to work on the forms. As he was taking measurements in the massive construction area for the No.1 Battleship, he soon realized that the forms were very different from anything he had ever worked with before. The first major difference was in the method of measurement. The engineers at Kure were not using metal tape measures, because the forms to be made from the ship's blueprint's were too large. With ordinary tape measures, which had to be moved along the length of the forms, small discrepancies in the length of individual tapes or minute changes in their length due to the expansion and contraction of the metal with changes in temperature could amount to large errors in measurement.

Another very unusual construction variant was the decision to leave out the layer of teak beneath the steel plates of the deck. In Baba's experience, teak planks between two and a half and four-centimeters thick were laid between the deck layers of a battleship. When the completed steel deck was attached to the hull, discrepancies could be corrected by planing down the teak, which thus acted as a buffer to correct small errors in the construction process.

Baba realized that by eliminating the teak layer, the designers were trying to reduce the weight of the ship, but because of the unusually large dimensions of the vessel, calculations on the forms would have to be extremely precise.

Although it was Baba's duty to give his subordinates moral support as they started the job of making the forms, he lacked confidence in his own ability to complete the job. He had only been shown a small portion of the battleship's plans, but from his long experience as a shipbuilding engineer, he could tell that the new vessel was preposterously large.

The deck plates for both the No. 1 and No. 2 battleships, which could only be formed through a state-of-the-art processing method, would be manufactured by the Kure steel mill. Another surprise was the thickness of the steel plates for the side of the ship: forty centimeters thick. Baba had heard that the plates used on the sides of the *Mutsu*, Japan's most heavily armored battleship to date, were thirty centimeters thick. Why, he wondered, with steel technology improving and armor getting stronger and thinner, were they building a vessel with plates over forty centimeters thick?

# 3
# Birth of a Titan

**Autumn 1933**

The first signs of what was to become the No. 2 Battleship project had begun to appear at Nagasaki Shipyard's No. 2 slipway as early as the autumn of 1933. That year the shipyard began to build huge gantry cranes that could be used in the construction of an unusually large vessel. These plans were closely intertwined with military and economic movements in Japan in the early 1930s.

The executives of the shipyard, who had been told of the Navy's plans to build new battleships in 1933, assumed that these would be relatively large vessels. They decided to expand the No. 2 shipbuilding slipway, the shipyard's largest, and construct giant gantry cranes, which would be mounted on two thick steel frames constructed along both sides of the slipway. The Navy was quickly informed of the shipyard's expansion plans and sent its official approval. The gantry cranes and slipway remodeling were an attempt by the shipyard to show the Navy that the yard was ready to build a large warship, and the shipyard took the Navy's approval as a green light for a new battleship project.

In early May 1935 the head of the Fourth Division of the Bureau of Naval Construction, Vice Admiral Mikinosuke Yamamoto, sent a coded telegram to President Kyosuke Tamai through the chief supervisor of naval construction. It read: "Urgent. Come to Tokyo at once."

Tamai was certain that Yamamoto wanted to talk about the construction of a new battleship. He left for Tokyo on the same day with Watanabe, the director of the shipyard's steel mill. When the two men arrived at the bureau's headquarters, Yamamoto questioned Tamai and Watanabe about the specific capabilities of the No. 2 slipway.

Only a few days after Tamai had returned to Nagasaki, Vice Admiral Teijiro Toyoda, vice chief of the General Affairs Department of the Bureau of Naval Construction, showed up unannounced at the shipyard with several naval engineers. Captain Hirata, Watanabe, and other senior shipyard executives were summoned to a secret meeting. On the conference table lay detailed plans of the No. 2 slipway, gantry cranes, and launching platform, and depth charts of Nagasaki Harbor and Nagasaki Bay.

Toyoda opened the meeting with a direct question: "Can you construct a warship with a maximum width of 124 feet on the No. 2 slipway?"

Watanabe and his colleagues looked at one another dumbfounded. The battleship *Nagato*, the largest ever built in Japan, had a maximum width of ninety-six feet. They could not imagine a battleship twenty-eight feet wider than that.

Watanabe tried to hide his surprise and glanced slowly over his research materials. "It is not impossible to build a ship of that size here," he said, "but it would create a tremendous strain on the gantry cranes. We would prefer that you set the width at 122 feet."

"But 124 feet is not impossible?" Toyoda pressed Watanabe.

"No, it's not impossible," Watanabe responded hesitantly.

"All right," Toyoda continued, "what is the maximum possible length for the battleship?"

Watanabe could not immediately answer Toyoda's question. He looked at his colleagues for support. A ship with a maximum width of ninety-six feet would have to be 700 feet long. With this ratio in mind, a battleship 124 feet wide would require a length of at least 1,000 feet. Vice President Ogawa had apparently made the same calculations as Watanabe.

Pointing at the plan in front of him, Ogawa explained, "If the battleship were 1,000 feet long, the bow would project out to here."

He indicated to a point far beyond the end of the slipway. "We would have to make a major cut through this hill and move the power room and other buildings over here. It would take a great deal of work. We would prefer it if you could keep the length to less than 850 feet."

Toyoda nodded slightly.

"It seems the ship you are planning is rather large..." Vice President Inagaki interjected.

Toyoda said nothing but turned to Watanabe and resumed his questioning. "Is the launch platform strong enough to take a battleship this size?"

"As it is now, no," Watanabe answered.

Judging from the specifications Toyoda had given for the battleship, Watanabe estimated that the vessel would weigh almost 50,000 tons. The launch platform could handle a ship the size of the *Tosa*. Anything heavier would probably cause it to collapse.

"I am also concerned that the ship may collide with the opposite shore of the harbor when it is launched," Toyoda said.

Nagasaki Harbor was extremely long and narrow. The shipyard was located on one side of the harbor, and the opposite shore was only 680 meters away from the No. 2 slipway. When a large ship was launched, the engineers worried that it might simply glide across the narrow harbor and crash into the opposite bank. With a launch weight of close to 50,000 tons, the ship might slide off with enough momentum to send it crashing into the far bank and right up onto the opposite shore.

Watanabe, who had launched a number of ships in Nagasaki Harbor, had done a great deal of research into ways of avoiding this problem. "Perhaps we could attach heavy chains to the battleship's port side," he suggested. "The weight of the ship would slow its speed, and the chains, by pulling the ship to the left, would prevent it from colliding with the far bank."

Toyoda nodded and smiled, and the conversation turned to other aspects of the launch.

When the construction was finished on a ship's hull, the rudders and screw propellers were attached and the ship set afloat. In preparation for the launch, the ship under construction was normally set on top of hundreds of thick wooden blocks. To slide the ship off the slipway, a launch platform the same length as the ship was constructed beneath the hull. The wooden blocks were then removed, and the weight of the ship was shifted onto the platform. The success of the entire operation depended on the strength of the launch structure.

"Can you build a launch platform thirteen feet wide?" Toyoda asked with concern.

The large scale of the vessel meant that an unusually wide launch platform was necessary to support its weight. Watanabe had already calculated that the platform would have to be an unprecedented thirteen feet wide. The launch platforms for the *Mutsu* and the U.S.S. *Lexington* had measured approximately seven feet. The largest launch platform used to date was for Britain's luxury liner the *Queen Mary*. It was ten and a half feet wide.

"No matter what technical problems may arise, we will use these plans as a basis for preparations," Ogawa answered.

After the meeting the shipyard executives discussed their displeasure with the situation among themselves. They had thought they had made all necessary preparations for the construction of a large warship, but the vessel the Navy had in mind was much larger than any of them had envisioned.

The Navy's expectations were not inconceivable from a technical standpoint, but the actual execution of the project would be difficult at best. Especially troubling was Watanabe's assertion that the outfitting dock was too shallow. He insisted it had to be at least ten meters deep. All the large-scale warships and commercial vessels built at the yard had been outfitted in this dock. The dock had been deep enough for all these vessels, and shipyard executives wondered what kind of ship could require a depth of ten meters.

Tamai held a series of meetings about the new battleship over the following several days. Because of Vice Admiral Toyoda's warning about the secrecy of the project, only three executives were permitted to attend: Inagaki, Ogawa, and Watanabe. They estimated it would take about two years to build the ship, from preparatory stages to launch. Outfitting would take an additional eighteen months.

The shipyard had to overcome several non-technical problems before construction could begin. The first of these was the serious shortage of manpower at the shipyard. The work force had fallen by two-thirds since the scrapping of the *Tosa*, and construction of a such a large vessel would be impossible with the present levels of manpower. On the other hand, the yard could now more readily handle the construction of a large warship. Improved facilities and more experienced workers had increased the yard's productivity, which meant that a work force thirty-five percent smaller than that working on the *Tosa* could perform about the same amount of work.

Still, the much larger scale of this new battleship made a personnel increase essential. Tamai obtained Mitsubishi head office's approval to employ 1,400 men as part of a first employee expansion program. The new workers would be trained by working on the battle cruiser *Tone*, then under construction at the shipyard, and the *Chikuma*, a second battle cruiser that was soon to be started.

Construction work on the *Chikuma* began on October 1, 1935. The cruiser was built on the No. 2 slipway to test the capacity of the gantry cranes. They performed flawlessly, and construction of the *Chikuma* went unusually well.

* * *

In December 1935 a naval disarmament conference opened in London. But on January 15, 1936, Japan withdrew from the talks. As the executives of the shipyard had predicted, a majority of Japan's leaders were in favor of allowing the Washington Treaty to lapse. Certain that the order to start building a new battleship was imminent, they planned the shipyard's second and third employee expansion programs.

The year 1936 was a portentous one for Japan, both domestically and internationally. In February a group of young army officers assassinated leading figures in the armed forces and cabinet in an attempt to overthrow the government. Although the revolt was suppressed after three days, it accelerated military involvement in national politics. In November Japan signed the Anti-Comintern Pact with Nazi Germany, followed by an alliance with Germany's ally, Italy.

The expansion of the gantry cranes for the No. 2 slipway were finished on schedule at the end of March. They loomed over the harbor like the legs of a giant iron-red crab. Partial renovations on the No. 2 slipway had already been completed in 1936, as a lure for the anticipated battleship contract.

Just as the citizens of Nagasaki were taking down the pine decorations from the New Year holidays on January 5, 1937, Tamai received an urgent telegram from Mitsubishi head office. The Bureau of Naval Construction in Tokyo had requested his presence at a meeting. Tamai rounded up Ogawa and Watanabe, and set off for Tokyo.

Attending the meeting from Mitsubishi head office were the president of Mitsubishi, Koyata Iwasaki, and the managing director, Tatsumi Ito. The Mitsubishi people waited in the the conference room for some time before the director of the Bureau of Naval Construction, Vice Admiral Muneshige Ueda, arrived with the chiefs of the Fourth Division and the General Affairs Division.

The admiral opened the meeting. "Because this project is a top military secret," he began, "I will inform you of it orally, without written documentation. The Navy has decided to start building two battleships of identical design. The first of these ships will be built at the Kure Naval Arsenal, the second at the Nagasaki Shipyard. I will explain the details of the project to you later, but I would like

25

the construction of both ships to be under the direction of the Kure Arsenal. The reason for your presence here today is to receive instructions concerning the No. 2 Battleship."

Iwasaki turned toward the Nagasaki executives, then said to Ueda, "We are delighted to accept your offer."

"We at the shipyard have to make preparations for the construction of this vessel," Tamai said. "Could you give us some specifics on the ship's displacement, length, and maximum width? A rough estimate will be fine."

"We're still not in a position to give you those specifications," Ueda answered. "We haven't reached a final decision about the design of the engines, but we would like you to begin making preparations for construction, while keeping in close contact with the Kure Arsenal."

The lack of concrete information about the ship left everyone unsure of how to proceed. The Bureau of Naval Construction did not provide any further instructions for several months after the Tokyo meeting, and in early March Tamai decided to send Watanabe to Kure to see how the arsenal was handling the preparations for the construction of the No.1 Battleship. Watanabe went to Kure with two engineers, but he returned to Nagasaki two days later, extremely disappointed with the outcome of his visit.

When Watanabe had approached Rear Admiral Kuwabara about the preparations the arsenal was making for the construction of the No. 1 Battleship, the rear admiral answered brusquely, "No. 1 Battleship? No. 2 Battleship? I don't know what you're talking about."

# 4

# Nowhere to Hide

**Spring 1937**

Tamai was not pleased to hear that his engineers had been treated so coldly by their supposed partners in Kure, when Rear Admiral Kuwabara should have known that the shipyard had already been given the go-ahead to begin readying its facilities for the No. 2 Battleship project. He reasoned that the only rationale for such behavior must be the extreme secrecy of the project.

In a rush of anxiety, he called a meeting in his office with vice presidents Inagaki and Ogawa, Watanabe, and engineers Koga and Yoshida. His purpose was to remind them that they were the only six people at the shipyard who knew of the No. 2 Battleship project and to keep it strictly secret.

As if to confirm Tamai's suspicions, the Bureau of Naval Construction ordered him to investigate methods of hiding the battleship during construction. Specific proposals were to be submitted as soon as possible.

Tamai was at a loss. Nagasaki Harbor is located at the bottom of the geographical equivalent of a bowl: It is surrounded on three sides by mountains. Nagasaki earned its reputation for beautiful scenery because of its elevation. The sloping streets overlook the harbor, where even today the Nagasaki Shipyard sprawls along the coast in full view of the city's residents.

Another problem was Nagasaki's large foreign population. In addition to the constant traffic of missionaries, the city had several Chinese communities, as well as British and American consulates. Nagasaki was also a terminus for the Shanghai Steamship Company.

The No. 2 slipway, where the ship would be built, could be seen easily from both land and sea. Tamai assigned Watanabe to the project, and Watanabe in turn asked engineers Isoe Takezawa and Shigeichi Koga to solve the problem.

Takezawa was not informed of the nature of the shipbuilding project he was working on: His brief was to hide a ship under construction on the No. 2 slipway. His first idea was to enclose the shipbuilding area and gantry cranes within a wall of galvanized aluminum plates. The proposed structure would be 40 meters wide, 270 meters long, and 36 meters high.

Koga found some basic flaws with this idea, however. An aluminum wall that size, even if it were technically possible to build it, would be vulnerable to high winds. In order to withstand Japan's seasonal typhoons, the shield would have to be porous—like the bamboo window screens of Japanese houses. But there were several other prerequisites: The screen had to be durable so as not to deteriorate during the three years it took to build and outfit the ship, and it would have to be fireproof, so as not to ignite from sparks given off by the welding guns.

Taking all of these factors into consideration, Takezawa and Koga began to test various materials. They first tested waterproofed cloth, which they cut into strips to lower wind resistance, but it was too light. Even a slight breeze would cause it to flutter uncontrollably.

The second material they tried was a specially reinforced bamboo screen. Thick bamboo rods were split lengthwise and strung together with rope. This, however, was far too heavy, and the engineers worried that the rope connecting the bamboo strips would eventually break.

Takezawa then suggested straw rope. Although the high water content of straw causes it to rot quickly, it would also naturally repel water and be a viable material for a slipway shield. But the undeniable drawback of straw, though, was its flammability.

The engineers tested a variety of materials for flammability in an abandoned factory and then asked the Design Department to calculate how much wind they could withstand. About one month into the testing they came up with the idea of using hemp. Hemp-palm rope was relatively heavy and would not fly away uncontrollably in the wind. It was strong and water resistant and did not rot easily (fishermen used it for anchor ropes and netting). Its low flammability also made it an ideal material for the slipway shield.

The test results on the hemp rope were extremely favorable, but Takezawa realized that the ship would be visible if the ropes were hung vertically from a frame. He decided to bind the ropes together and hang them horizontally like the slats of a window blind. Watanabe was satisfied that the hemp idea was workable and reported the results to Tamai and Captain Hirata. Once they had received the approval of the Bureau of Naval Construction, Koga and Takezawa calculated the amount of hemp palm needed to shield the slipway. In order to hinder visibility at close range, they decided to build a three-meter aluminum wall around the construction area. The hemp blinds would be hung from the gantry cranes, with two or three blinds overlapping in high-security areas.

If the blinds were fifteen meters by ten meters, about 500 blinds would be needed to enclose the entire slipway. To produce 75,000 square meters of hemp screen, they would need 2,500 kilometers of rope, which would weigh 400 tons. Even more hemp rope would be required to hide the ship during the outfitting stage after the hull had been launched. Watanabe was overwhelmed by the amount of hemp needed for the project and wondered if the shipyard could really buy enough rope in time for the start of construction. He thought the only possible way would be to use the shipyard's rigging plant to manufacture the blinds, but then it would quickly become known that the shipyard was buying massive quantities of hemp-palm rope. If it was at all possible, he did not want anyone to know about the hemp until after construction on the ship had started.

Watanabe conferred with Tamai and suggested that the shipyard buy raw hemp fiber and process it on site. Tamai ordered the general affairs director to make an urgent purchase of 500 tons of hemp palm, calculating for weight loss after processing. A list was made up of hemp-palm distributors and warehouses in Kyushu, and the director of the Materials Division was put in charge of gathering the fibers. He told the five men he had ordered to buy the hemp that all transactions were to be made in cash and were to be kept secret. The men set off for Kyushu the next day to make their purchases.

\* \* \*

In mid-May the naval arsenal at Kure requested that some engineers from Nagasaki come for consultations about the construction of the No. 2 Battleship.

This time Watanabe was given a very different welcome by Rear Admiral Kuwabara. "We've begun making the model forms for the No.1 Battleship," he said, "and we thought it was time we let your people in on it."

In October 1934 the Naval General Staff had asked the Bureau of Naval Construction to present concrete proposals for the construction of two new battleships. Lieutenant Commander Keiji Fukuda made the preliminary study. Weighing the pros and cons of twenty-three different proposals, the bureau had not decided on the final design until March 1937—two and a half years later.

The design process included eleven of the Navy's top specialists: six shipbuilding designers, three engine designers, an ordnance designer, and a deck designer. The basic plans were drawn by thirty-five-year-old Lieutenant Commander Shigeru Makino, who had been transferred to the arsenal, where he headed the Shipbuilding Department's Design Division. Makino, who had once taught at Tokyo Imperial University, was one of the Navy's finest engineers.

"When you visited last June we were having problems with the design of the engines," Kuwabara said.

The design for combined diesel-steam engines had only been finalized at the end of July. Two of the four propulsion axles for the screw propellers would be diesel powered and two would be steam powered.

"The track record for diesel vessels, like the *Taigei*, the *Tsurugisaki*, and the *Takasaki,* is shameful," Kuwabara went on. "There have been too many engine failures. So we decided to equip these ships with four turbines, which delayed the final decision on the overall design. I knew the Nagasaki Shipyard had been given instructions to prepare for the construction of the No. 2 Battleship, but circumstances did not allow me to discuss any details with you when you last visited. Please forgive the cold reception."

Watanabe was then taken on a tour of the arsenal. The floor of the dry dock for the No. 1 Battleship had been dug deeper to accommodate the vessel's unusual size, and enormous gantry cranes were under construction. Watanabe's discussions with Kuwabara that day touched on some of the details of the battleship project. Construction of the No. 2 Battleship would be carried out to the specifications of Makino's design. The extra-thick steel plates needed for the battleship's armor would be sent from the arsenal's steel mill.

Just as Watanabe was about to leave, Kuwabara said, "Sometime later this month we will send you the basic blueprints for the No. 2 Battleship. Get ready at your end, and we'll give you as much help as we possibly can."

# 5
# Fear at Midnight

**Summer 1937**

On July 1, 1937, Nagasaki Shipyard executives received the long-awaited blueprints and specifications of the No. 2 Battleship from the Bureau of Naval Construction.

Watanabe, Tamai, Inagaki, and Ogawa silently read through the specifications and studied the blueprints, all of which were stamped "Top Secret."

> Length: 263 meters
> Maximum Width: 38.9 meters
> Water Displacement
> (standard): 68,200 tons
> (full load): 71,100 tons
> Maximum Crude Oil Capacity: 6,300 tons
> Maximum Navigable Distance (at 16 knots):
> 7,200 nautical miles (13,334 kilometers)
> Maximum Speed: 27 knots (50 kilometers per hour)
> Horsepower: 150,000 HP
> 9 Main Guns: 46 centimeters (18.1 inches)
> 15 Auxiliary Guns: 15.5 centimeters (6.1 inches)
> Aircraft: 6
> Crew: 2,300

Every single figure quoted far exceeded the specifications of any vessel the Nagasaki Shipyard had ever built. The water displacement for the No. 2 Battleship had originally been estimated at

50,000 tons, but the figure in the specifications surpassed that by 20,000 tons.

The No. 2 Battleship was to be fifty meters longer than the 214-meter British battleship HMS *Nelson* and the 213-meter Japanese battleship *Nagato*. It was more than ten meters wider then either the *Nelson* (thirty-two meters) or the *Nagato* (twenty-nine meters). But to reduce the target area offered to enemy craft, the overall length of the ship had been shortened, giving it an unusual configuration for a battleship. The vessel's extraordinary width was necessary to accommodate its nine enormous main guns and to withstand the recoil from their simultaneous firing.

Believing that the value of a ship was determined largely by its firepower, every navy wanted its battleships to be capable of inflicting greater damage on more distant targets. The No. 2 Battleship's nine forty-six-centimeter guns would be the largest ever mounted on a battleship. A single forty-six-centimeter cannon had reportedly been mounted onto the British cruiser HMS *Furious*. When it had been test fired, the recoil had severely damaged the ship's hull. The main guns would also be the the longest in shipbuilding history at twenty-one meters.

The four men stared at the blueprints in silence. Tamai was the first to speak. Standing up with a stunned look, he muttered, "We've got to go through with it. The Navy trusted our engineering expertise enough to give us this project. We've got to get started immediately."

Tamai assigned individual duties to the men sworn in on the project. He created a No. 2 Battleship Construction Office to oversee the project, made Watanabe its director, and designated Shigeichi Koga as his assistant. Several other engineers and executives needed for the project swore the oath of secrecy and were given jobs in the new office.

Shortly afterwards Watanabe called the first engineering conference of the Construction Office's new appointees.

"Construction of a large battleship is expected to begin in the next six months," he began. "The specifics of the project are a military secret, and I cannot describe them in detail at present. Please do not try to find out more than you already know. I want you all to concentrate on the specific duties assigned to you."

The preparatory work for the project fell into two categories: the expansion of shipyard facilities and the engineering research necessary to build the No. 2 Battleship.

The most urgent work to be done in improving facilities was the expansion and reinforcement of the No. 2 slipway and gantry cranes. In order to accommodate a 263-meter-long battleship, the slipway would have to be lengthened by sixty meters on its inland side. The unprecedented 38.9-meter maximum width of the battleship called for an eight- to fifteen-meter expansion in the width of the slipway where the central portion of the battleship would be built. Enormous quantities of steel would have to be used to reinforce the aft portion of the slipway, so that it could withstand the weight of the ship during the launch.

However, the remodelling work on the slipway could not begin until the battle cruiser *Chikuma*, then under construction on the No. 2 slipway, had been launched. Watanabe decided that the only possible course was to begin cutting into the hill behind the slipway and procuring the steel necessary for the reinforcement.

The engineering research necessary for the No. 2 Battleship project was another area of concern. One of the most difficult problems Watanabe foresaw was the launch. The Kure Arsenal had already solved many of the engineering problems in building the No. 1 Battleship, but the launch presented a more difficult challenge in Nagasaki than in Kure. The No. 1 Battleship was to be constructed in a huge dry dock. When the time came to launch the ship, water would be pumped into the dock, and the hull would be towed into the harbor by tugs.

In Nagasaki, the engineers would have to find a way to slide the ship into the harbor from the sloping slipway. It would be extremely difficult to get a vessel as heavy as the No. 2 Battleship to slide smoothly. In the past there had been several near launch failures from the No. 2 slipway. The hull could capsize and be damaged beyond repair, or it could even injure and kill workers if it began to slide before the prescribed time. Additionally, the project was a top military secret, and the shipyard could not freely undertake preparations for the launch.

Trying to pick the right person for this difficult job, Watanabe immediately thought of Joshichi Omiya, one of his new subordinates in the No. 2 Battleship Construction Office. Omiya was a graduate of the Mitsubishi Engineering School and an experienced shipbuilding engineer. He had almost a hero's reputation in Nagasaki as the yard's launch expert. Watanabe thought that he was the only man who could carry off what promised to be a troublesome launch.

Watanabe summoned Omiya to his office immediately, had him swear the oath of secrecy, then explained the details of the project. The two engineers then put their heads together to select a third man to help with the pre-launch research. They chose an ambitious young engineer named Takeshi Hamada.

In the months following July 1937 communication between the Nagasaki Shipyard and the Kure Arsenal became more frequent. Several teams of shipyard engineers were sent to Kure. Following official instructions, they told their colleagues and families that they were going to Hiroshima on business.

In early fall the Kure Arsenal sent a partial set of blueprints for the No. 2 Battleship to Nagasaki. Then in mid-October a commercial freighter called the *Shirogane* sailed from Kure and made an unscheduled stop at Nagasaki. After the freighter had docked inside the shipyard, cranes lifted its canvas-wrapped cargo ashore. This consisted of sixty-eight steel plates to be laid under the munitions chambers. Workers stored the plates in a warehouse without removing the covers.

With the arrival of the first shipment of materials for the new battleship, a sense of urgency was transmitted from the arsenal to the shipbuilding team in Nagasaki. In order to maintain smooth

35

communications with the arsenal, Watanabe made frequent trips to Kure. With each visit he could sense the imminent start of construction in the tension of the engineers who were working around the clock to finish preparations.

The military police inside the arsenal stepped up their patrols. Workers began constructing a roof over the dry dock where the battleship was to be built in order to shield it from view. It seemed to Watanabe that the strain on the faces of the officers at Kure increased with each visit.

In Nagasaki, workers had begun cutting into the hillside behind the No. 2 slipway, and the shipyard's rigging plant was busily manufacturing the hemp screens that would be used to hide the ship. Workers puzzled about what the odd hemp screens would be used for. Some said it was a net to keep enemy submarines out of the bay, others that it was a mine net that would be floated on the harbor.

At the beginning of November the Kure Arsenal informed Watanabe that construction on the world's largest battleship had begun quietly with a small gathering of informed personnel at the dock. On the same day Watanabe was called to office of the chief supervisor of naval construction.

"With construction started on the No. 1 Battleship," Captain Hirata said, "construction on the No. 2 Battleship is just around the corner. I want to step up security inside the shipyard."

Sentries were posted at all gates of the shipyard to prevent the entry of unauthorized personnel. More and more shipyard workers took the oath of secrecy, and soon over 300 men were in on the military secret. At first they were allowed to roam freely about the plant and could not be distinguished from the workers who did not know about the project. But realizing that one slip-up could create serious security problems, shipyard management decided that it was vital to find a way to differentiate employees who had taken the oath from the rest of the workers.

In a meeting with senior shipyard executives, Hirata explained how the informed could be distinguished from the uninformed.

"I've already discussed this idea with Bureau of Naval Construction, and I want you to implement it right away," the captain said. "In order to distinguish those who know about the project from the rest of the workers, armbands will be issued to those employees who have sworn the oath. Two types of armbands will be made: one for engineers and administrators and one for manual workers. Each armband will be numbered, and employees must be required to wear them at all times.

"A book containing employees' photographs will be made up and checked each morning before the armbands are issued. The book will be checked again at night when the armbands are returned.

"Workers who have taken the oath of secrecy must not be allowed to roam freely about the shipyard. The area around the slipway, the storage area for steel plating, the blueprint area, and the Design Department must be designated top-security areas and police patrols there increased. The only individuals who should be permitted to go in and out of these areas are those who have special permission from me."

Watanabe took immediate steps to comply with Hirata's orders. Three days later he had the armbands distributed to all workers who had sworn the oath. From that day on security was stepped up at the main gate and military police, whose number had been increasing over the weeks, could be seen throughout the shipyard. Only a few of the uninformed workers were permitted to move freely about the shipyard.

Once out of the shipyard gates, the peace of Nagasaki's streets was like another world. With the tourist season long over, there were few visitors in the city. Winter arrived, but the spell of warm weather continued. An occasional church bell would ring, or a long file of citizens waving flags would march to Nagasaki Station to see off young soldiers going to the China front, but even this did not disturb the tranquility of the city.

The citizens of Nagasaki did not notice at first, but subtle changes were taking place around them. The number of military policemen stationed on the hills around Nagasaki suddenly increased, and the city was visited by a large detachment of detectives from the secret police. These men had been picked from among Japan's most experienced officers—some coming from as far away as Osaka and Tokyo. Their task was to keep a special watch on foreign residents, tourists, and shipyard employees. They had received special training to pass as ordinary civilians, and several of them got jobs as taxi and bus drivers.

The townspeople were unaware of their presence until December 12, 1937. On that winter night sixty detectives gathered at Nagasaki police headquarters. Arming themselves with pistols, they left quietly from the back of the building and made their way through the city's unlit alleyways toward Chinatown.

At about 1:00 A.M. they began a thorough search of every Chinese house they could find, dragging all adult males into the street and herding them back to police headquarters. The men were held overnight in a police gymnasium and called out one by one the following day for questioning.

The police told the Chinese that they had been arrested on suspicion of spying, and each was asked what he was doing in Nagasaki. The interrogations continued with specifics that only confused the already dazed Chinese.

"What, beside commercial vessels, are they building at the Nagasaki Shipyard? What is behind the Glover Estate?"

Frightened by the rough treatment, the detainees could only answer that they did not know.

Everyone in Nagasaki knew that the shipyard was involved in building naval vessels, and the fact that there was an army camp on the mountain behind the Glover Estate was also common knowledge. The detectives repeated the questions relentlessly, shouting at the Chinese and throwing them to the floor until they passed out. The detainees were finally released two months later. One elderly man had died under police torture.

Similar investigations were carried out throughout Kyushu during that period. Any person who was determined to be "undesirable" during the crackdown was ordered to leave the country. Police crammed Chinese nationals onto ships and deported them back to the continent. Two ships carrying 350 Chinese each sailed from Miike bound for Shanghai, and about 1,000 more Chinese were deported from Moji.

News of the incident quickly spread around Nagasaki, a city where foreigners traditionally blended in with the Japanese population. Many Japanese residents of the city pleaded for the release of the Chinese detainees. The police responded by putting them on a list of persons requiring special supervision.

# 6

# The Monster's Backbone

**Spring 1938**

When the Nagasaki Shipyard began making model forms from the blueprints sent from Kure, Watanabe was faced with a new dilemma. It was his responsibility to decide how to store and distribute the top-secret blueprints from the arsenal, as well as those from his own design department, without losses or information leaks.

The Navy had classified the blueprints into four categories: top military secret, military secret, top secret, and secret. Watanabe was not concerned about materials classified military secret or above because Etsushi Sakakibara, the chief of the Design Department, kept them in one of the shipyard's safes. The problem for Watanabe was how to manage the documents classified military secret and secret. Engineers would need large numbers of blueprints to build the vessel (the shipyard ended up drafting 31,380 such documents before the project's completion), and in order to ensure a smooth production process, the blueprints would have to be sent to various divisions of the shipyard. The loss of even one blueprint could cause an insoluble problems not only for the shipyard but also for the Navy. After consulting with Captain Hirata, Watanabe decided to order a complete renovation of the office where the blueprints would be stored.

A top-security room was planned for the third floor of the shipyard's administration building. The one entrance to this windowless concrete bunker would be guarded day and night. Half of the room would be given over to desks for the engineers and blueprinters assigned to copy the blueprints, and the remaining half to a blue-print storage area surrounded by a strong metal cage.

An administrator would be responsible for the storage and filing of the documents, and only he would have the key to the blueprint lockers. He would be required to pass the documents out of the cage via a small slot in the steel mesh.

Watanabe decided that the only people who should be allowed to enter the room, besides the engineers and blueprinters working there, would be himself and a few other high-ranking executives and Navy officers.

Remodeling work began immediately. The director of the Design Department, Sakakibara, was put in overall charge of the Blueprint Division. The ultimate responsibility for the caged blueprint library was given to Yasusada Kita, an employee known for his strict discipline.

In February Lieutenant Commander Masao Kajiwara was assigned to the office of the supervisor of naval construction. An experienced engineer, Kajiwara was a graduate of Tokyo Imperial University's Department of Marine Engineering. He had studied in the United States for two years and was a member of the team that had conducted the test firings on the hull of the *Tosa*. After planning the construction of the hull of the No. 1 Battleship, he went to Nagasaki to supervise the building of the No. 2 Battleship.

Kajiwara's appointment to the project was a godsend for Watanabe, not only on the technical side, but also because he could now expect much smoother communications with Kure.

At about the same time the Sales Department of Mitsubishi and the Nagasaki Shipyard entered into final negotiations with the Bureau of Naval Construction on the contract for the No. 2 Battleship. As a commercial enterprise, the shipyard treated the contract for the No. 2 Battleship just like any other order. No matter how important the battleship was to the nation, each project undertaken by the yard had to show a profit for the company.

Tamai entrusted these negotiations to Yonejiro Mori, head of the

Sales Department's Warship Division and a graduate of Tokyo Commercial High School (now Hitotsubashi University). A veteran of many negotiations with the Navy, Mori had a reputation as a stubborn bargainer. He was able to smile with his Navy counterparts and ply them with small talk, but he always managed to safeguard the company's business interests. Because Mori had the trust of the Navy, he could wrap up deals in half the time needed by the shipyard's other negotiators, without making any financial compromises.

Mori put together a written estimate for the No. 2 Battleship, which he submitted to the Bureau of Naval Construction. The two sides started negotiations using Mori's estimate. But it soon came out that the budget for the No. 1 and No. 2 battleships had already been set by the Finance Ministry and approved by the Diet. If the Navy had asked for the full amount needed to build the two battleships, it would have given away their size. Instead, the Navy Ministry had asked for a budget to build two 35,000-ton vessels, explaining that any weaknesses in the fleet because of the relatively small scale of the new vessels would be compensated for by the construction of aircraft carriers, destroyers, and submarines.

Mori and the head of Mitsubishi's Sales Department visited the Bureau of Naval Construction daily. The Navy negotiators would break down Mori's estimate into small items and try to coax him into lowering his prices.

"The estimate is much too high," the Navy side would complain.

Mori remained humble but unmoved. "We have given you the lowest possible figure for the work," Mori would counter. "We need that amount at the very least. The figures you're suggesting not only rob us of any profit, they put us in the red."

"You keep talking about profit. We want you to think a little more about the significance of this project," the Navy men responded.

"It is difficult for us to demand money in these circumstances," Mori replied. "We understand only too well the significance of the work we are doing. Nevertheless, the Nagasaki Shipyard is part of a civilian company. We must consider the livelihoods of our employees and our responsibility to our stockholders. If we don't manage to make a small profit, the very future of the company is at stake."

Negotiations remained at an impasse until a final round was called with the senior officers of the Bureau of Naval Construction and top executives from Mitsubishi attending. The Navy finally accepted the Mitsubishi proposal with minor revisions, and the thirty-clause contract was signed on February 10.

Items, such as "Contracted cost of the No. 2 Battleship: 52.65 million yen," "Completion date: March 31, 1942," and "Place of delivery to the Navy: Nagasaki," took up most of the document, but almost all were changed after the contract was signed. The final amount the Navy agreed to pay the Nagasaki Shipyard for the No. 2 Battleship was 64.9 million yen—less than half the budget estimated by the Kure Arsenal for construction of the No. 1 Battleship.

The contract for the No. 2 Battleship stipulated that major parts of the ship, such as the armor plating, ordnance, and engines, would be supplied free of charge by the Navy. The Navy also changed the No. 2 Battleship's delivery site to Kure.

The date of completion was postponed only two months after the contract was signed, via a coded message from the Bureau of Naval Construction:

Top Secret
   Due to budget considerations, the contracted delivery date of March 31, 1942, is hereby revised to December 28, 1942.
Date: April 10, 1938.
Bureau of Naval Construction
Chief of the Accounts Department
Shiro Takahashi

The Navy had picked this seemingly arbitrary new date because

March 31 was the end of the fiscal year for the Diet budget. It was an obvious attempt on the Navy Ministry's part to hide the full cost of the new battleships from the Finance Ministry.

The battle cruiser *Chikuma* was launched from the No. 2 slipway on March 19, 1938. The slipway stood vast and empty, surrounded on both sides by its huge gantry cranes. The next day brought a frenzy of preparatory work for the new battleship. After workers had removed the launching platform used to slide the *Chikuma* into the harbor, the concrete surface of the No. 2 slipway was left bare and ready for construction to begin.

Workers erected a three-meter-high aluminum wall around the outer perimeter of the slipway and began to hang hemp blinds from the gantry cranes to a height of ten meters.

Construction on the No. 2 Battleship officially began at 10:00 A.M. on March 29, 1938. Traditionally, hundreds of people would have been invited to attend, but in this case only Captain Hirata, President Tamai, and another twenty people were present on the slipway.

The simple ceremony consisted of a toast of cold saké. Afterwards Watanabe stood on the No. 2 slipway and looked up at the clouds overhead. According to the construction schedule, he had only two years and seven months before the battleship would be launched. In that time a huge fortress of steel would be standing on the empty expanse of concrete around him. He could not make himself believe that such an unimaginably large battleship could ever be completed in such a short period of time under his direction. In the center of the slipway lay a portion of the massive keel—the backbone of the battleship. To Watanabe the unfamiliar hunk of metal seemed like the backbone of a monster.

# 7

# The First Rivet

**Spring 1938**

About twenty days after the start of construction workers began riveting the transverse members of the ship's hull. Watanabe and Koga carefully supervised the installation of the first of the massive four-centimeter rivets to be used on the battleship.

Before the No. 1 and No. 2 battleships were conceived, the largest rivets used in warship construction were 1.5 centimeters in diameter, though on rare occasions 2.8-centimeter rivets had been used. The No. 2 Battleship required a massive number of four-centimeter rivets. In addition to the fact that the rivets were unusually large and difficult to handle, the unusual thickness of the battleship's armor plates made traditional riveting methods impossible. For this reason, the rivets had to be extremely hard and exceptionally precise in size.

Almost a year earlier Watanabe had asked engineer Takezawa to research possible production techniques for four-centimeter rivets. Relying on the Kure Arsenal for information and guidance, Takezawa had initially manufactured 16,000 rivets. In the end he used none of them. Instead, he was forced to use rivets forged slightly larger than needed and tapered to the correct size one by one.

Takezawa also faced problems designing the riveting gun to drive the rivets into the steel plating. For the No. 1 Battleship, the Kure Arsenal used a giant rivet gun specially made for the project by the Uryu Engineering Company in Osaka. With this gun as a model, Takezawa designed and manufactured a gun for the No. 2 Battleship. The first rivet went in with a solid bang—a good sign for the start of the project.

As construction progressed, the same kind of hemp blinds that enclosed the No. 2 slipway were used to shield the neighboring No. 1 slipway, which was used to store construction materials, including the large steel plates needed for the hull. The massive hemp blinds cast a dreary shadow inside the slipway, and on windy days they would flap heavily against the frames of the gantry cranes.

* * *

Once the project was under way Koga and Kajiwara began taking weekly walks in the mountains overlooking the harbor. The two men would hike to an elevated spot with a good view of the shipyard and train their binoculars on the No. 2 slipway and the surrounding area. They also took photographs using a telephoto lens to estimate the visibility of the slipway interior through the screens. They also needed to check periodically to make sure the hemp screens were high enough to hide the increasing height of the battleship.

Every time they took their walks, the two men were stopped and questioned by the military police. At first both men presented their identity cards, but they were soon recognized by most of the policemen, who would stop for casual chats. One of the officers told Koga and Kajiwara that all civilians hiking in the area were arrested and questioned by the secret police.

On another occasion a young police officer asked Kajiwara, "By the way, commander, they're hanging some strange things up at the shipyard. They look almost like some kind of straw matting. Do you know what it is?"

Koga was aware that the screens had become a regular topic of conversation among the citizens of Nagasaki. Looking down at the shipyard, he realized that the brown screens did not exactly blend in with their surroundings. He could only respond to the officer's question with a smile.

Kajiwara gave the officer a sharp look and reprimanded him. "Your duty is to patrol the area. Don't concern yourself about things that don't concern you!"

The surprised young officer backed away and let them pass. Kajiwara walked a good distance from the officer before turning to Koga. "You have to be strict with curious people," he said with a grin, "We can't count on the military police to keep this project secret. The way things are now, you can get a good view of the ship from any one of these hilltops. The geography of the city is our worst enemy."

Kajiwara stopped and both men looked down into the shipyard.

"Maybe we should build observation posts to supervise the area a little more discreetly," Kajiwara said. His face lit up as he was struck with his first surefire idea for keeping inquisitive eyes away from the battleship. "They should have a clear view of not only the mountains, but of the city and the beach as well. We'll arrest any person we catch looking at the shipyard or taking photographs of it."

"We'll have to do that at the very least," Koga said. "At the moment the battleship can be seen from anywhere in Nagasaki. The observation posts will have to be in locations with a clear view of the harbor."

"No," Kajiwara replied, "We wouldn't get a thorough enough effect. We have to establish several surveillance posts around the shipyard itself. We'll station guards at the posts and have them look out at the mountains, city, and coast. Any location from which it is possible for someone to spy on the battleship must also be visible from the shipyard."

Kajiwara sent a man to the Sasebo Naval Station to borrow three pairs of twelve-centimeter binoculars. These were installed at observation posts inside the shipyard. Koga tested the binoculars by scanning the surrounding mountains. Through the high-magnification binoculars not only could he distinguish details on the clothing of people walking in town and of the secret police patrolling the hills, but he could even make out their faces and spot small animals in the mountains.

The binoculars would also be trained on the vessels traveling in and out of Nagasaki Harbor. Several ferries made daily runs from Nagasaki to the various small islands in the bay. These ships passed close by the No. 2 slipway. Kajiwara sent a special request to the police, asking them to dispatch officers onto the ferries to black out the windows on the shipyard side.

\* \* \*

In June the famous Peiron Boat Races are held in Nagasaki Harbor. Half a dozen decorated fishing boats, each crewed by 30 oarsmen, race across the harbor to the sound of drums and gongs. Tourists throng to the city to see the event.

That year, however, only a few days before the event, the police informed the fishermen that the race would have to be held outside the harbor. Traditionally the event started in Nagasaki Bay, but then the boats raced toward the finish line at the harbor's innermost point. The closer the race was to the city, the more spectators it would attract, which is what the fishermen wanted.

The reason given for the ban was the danger of collisions with larger vessels. The organizers of the festival complained, but police orders could not be ignored. The festival was held outside Nagasaki Harbor and attracted a very small crowd.

Increased police patrols around the city and the restrictions on the local festival had a repressive effect on the citizens of Nagasaki. The measures aroused everyone's curiosity as to what kind of vessel was being built in the shipyard, and made them wonder why it was so important.

Naturally, attention focused on the No. 2 slipway because of the strange hemp screens, and townspeople asked friends who worked at the shipyard what was being built behind them. Most employees had no idea, and the ones who did know remained stubbornly silent. As a result, rumors abounded: Some said the shipyard was building a submarine, others, a giant aircraft carrier.

# 8

# The Lost Blueprint

**Summer 1938**

Construction on the battleship progressed smoothly as spring turned to summer. On the No. 2 slipway, the giant cranes lifted building materials into place, and the sound of riveting filled the air.

The hemp blinds surrounding the slipway climbed skyward, as the hull of the ship began to take shape. With poor ventilation in the summer, the work area soon resembled a steam bath. Workers grit their teeth and suffered through the heat and stale air, waiting for the relief of autumn.

Toward the end of July a crisis occurred that triggered panic among the shipyard's executives and Navy personnel: A top-secret blueprint disappeared without trace.

At about 5:00 P.M. on an otherwise normal working day, the administrator of the top-security room discovered that one of the No. 2 Battleship blueprints had not been handed in. There was only one entrance to the concrete top-security room. The engineers in the drafting area borrowed blueprints from the storage cage when working copies of the originals were required at the construction site. After copying, the originals were immediately returned to the administrator.

The six engineers and two blueprinters in the drafting area had just returned the originals to the administrator in the storage area. Checking each blueprint against a master list, the administrator quickly realized that one was missing. Flustered, he flipped back through his records to see if it could have been left in the drafting area. Neither the records nor the ensuing search turned up the document.

After the fruitless thirty-minute search, the six engineers and two blueprinters were prevented from returning home that evening. The guard then locked the doors and ran to fetch Yasusada Kita, the man in charge of the top-security room. Kita was stunned by the news. He immediately told Sakakibara, the head of the Design Department, and soon the news reached Watanabe and Tamai.

Tamai ran to tell Captain Hirata, and both men dashed to the Design Department. When they arrived Hirata gave Tamai a brusque warning not to enter the security area. Hirata, who had grown very close to Tamai and the other shipyard executives during the planning stages of the project, suddenly drew the line on congeniality with shipyard personnel and concentrated on his responsibilities as a Navy officer.

He had the guard unlock the doors and entered the room with his subordinates. "What type of plan is missing?" he asked the administrator.

He was far from pleased with the answer: The lost blueprint showed a section of the turret that rotated the battleship's main guns.

An experienced engineer needed only to see this partial design to calculate the size of the entire turret, as well as the scale of the massive main guns to be mounted on the ship. From there he would easily realize that these guns were far larger than the standard forty-centimeter guns usually fitted on battleships.

All of the engineers and blueprinters in the division were forced to strip. Their clothes were searched, their desks were ransacked, and the room was scoured from one end to the other, but the blueprint was not found.

The top-security room was completely sealed off from the rest of the building, and its only entrance was a guarded steel door. When an employee in the room wanted to go to the toilet, he was obliged to check out of the security area and sign his name in a record book. When he returned he had to go through the same procedure. At lunchtime the employees in the drafting area were required to return the blueprints they had been working on to the administrator, and once everyone had left for lunch, the guard locked the door. The security checks on personnel entering and exiting the room seemed foolproof.

Inspections of the blueprints themselves were also unusually thorough. Kita went over instructions on security procedures two or three times a month with the administrators and drafting staff. Every evening an administrator would inspect the blueprints in the storage area and report to the shipyard's president. Navy personnel would visit the storage area at least once a month to inspect the blueprints, and the top-security room three or four times a month to look things over. The day before the incident Hirata had conducted one of his surprise inspections and determined that nothing was suspicious or out of place.

Each of the designs had been accounted for before they were handed out of the storage area after lunch, leading Hirata to surmise that the blueprint had gone missing between 1:00 P.M. and 5:00 P.M.

Only two outsiders had entered the security room that day according to the record kept by the guard. Watanabe had visited the room that morning with Baba, who had just returned from Kure. Watanabe had announced his visit in advance, and the Design Department was expecting him. Both Watanabe and Baba had entered and left the room in the morning and therefore could not have had anything to do with the missing document.

Hirata summoned all employees working in the room and said, "The lost blueprint is a high-level military secret. Its location is a matter of grave national importance, and may even affect the survival of our nation. The design cannot simply have disappeared. I am sorry to say that I can not permit any of you to return home. If someone in this group knows where the blueprint is, please speak up now." He looked at them coldly as he spoke.

The engineers and blueprinters were tense, and an uncomfortable hush filled the room. Hirata turned around and walked out.

Outside the security area, Hirata whispered instructions to Tamai, who nodded nervously. One of Hirata's subordinates left hurriedly, and a few minutes later the commander of the military police arrived with several men.

The MPs lead the six engineers and two blueprinters out of the security room, down the stairs of the Design Department building, and into khaki-colored cars, which took them out of the shipyard and along the Nagasaki coast road.

Hirata ordered Kajiwara to send a coded telegram to the Bureau of Naval Construction, then he called together the top executives of the shipyard to decide how to deal with the problem.

Two men were assigned to the investigation: Kajiwara from the Navy and Sakakibara from the shipyard. Each man would choose people from his own staff to investigate the whereabouts of the missing blueprint. It was also decided that the number of investigators should be limited to fifty men, to prevent news of the loss from leaking outside the plant.

By dawn the following morning the investigators had confirmed that the blueprint was not anywhere in the top-security room. The doors of the room were locked and sealed, and the search was extended to the other offices of the Design Department.

That evening Commander Sato of the Bureau of Naval Construction arrived at the shipyard. He winced when he was told that the blueprint had still not been located. He asked about the type of blueprint lost and conditions inside the top-security room before and after the incident, and immediately sent a detailed report to Tokyo.

What the Navy was most afraid of was that, if the blueprint fell into foreign hands, its greatest rival in the Pacific, the U.S. Navy, would have a general idea of the designs of the No. 1 and No. 2 battleships. The U.S. Navy was faced with a limit to the size of its battleships because of the width of the Panama Canal—its link between the Atlantic and the Pacific. The Japanese were hoping to take advantage of this weakness by building a fleet of giant battle-ships equipped with forty-six-centimeter guns. They were hoping that this overwhelming difference in battleship capability would help them defeat the U.S. Navy in the event of a war. For this reason, the secrecy of the No. 1 and No. 2 battleships was considered to be vital to Japan's military survival.

Sato called another meeting with the naval supervisors and top executives of the shipyard to explain to them the gravity of the situation. He ordered them to locate the blueprint—at any cost.

Each room in the Design Department was searched again several times, as well as the offices of the shipyard president, the director of the project, and each of the department chiefs. When even this failed to turn up the lost blueprint, investigators widened their search to the General Affairs Department and the Sales Department, which actually had little to do with construction of the battleship.

The Bureau of Naval Construction considered the loss of the blueprint to be a gross dereliction of duty on the part of the Navy personnel attached to the shipyard. Captain Hirata and his men realized that suicide would be the only recourse if they could not locate the blueprint. Even suicide would not erase their guilt and carelessness in permitting such an incident to occur.

Shipyard executives would be held responsible to an even higher degree than the naval supervisors because of their direct responsibility for the project. Although they were civilians with civilian responsibilities, they had taken an oath of secrecy and accepted special commissions as Navy officers. They too would naturally have to accept full responsibility for the incident. The president and his subordinates would be forced to accept imprisonment and severe military punishment.

The morning after they were led away from the shipyard by the military police, the eight employees who were suspected of stealing the blueprint were divided into two groups. One was taken to Nagasaki police headquarters and the other to the harbor police station. At each of the facilities, the most seasoned officers of the secret police awaited the arrival of the suspects.

The eight men were held in separate cells and questioned one at a time. The six engineers and two blueprinters had been appointed to their posts because they were considered to be Nagasaki Shipyard's finest. Their characters and backgrounds had been strictly investigated by the authorities before they were assigned to the top-security room. But this fact meant nothing to the police interrogators, whose only concern was that a blueprint had disappeared.

The officers had decided that because of the special security in force in the top-security room, the perpetrator of the crime had to be one of the eight men working there. The police conducted thorough searches of each of the men's homes, as well as carefully rechecking their backgrounds to see if any of them had close relationships with suspicious third parties—especially foreigners —and whether any of them were in any financial difficulties or had covert relationships with women.

Investigators looked into every detail of the lives of the eight suspects, and used the results of their investigations to question them. If they found the slightest discrepancy between an employee's account and the information they had obtained through their investigations, they tortured him until they got an explanation.

In the course of their interrogations, the investigators struck the suspects with bamboo rods, slapped them in the face, for the sake of "accurate questioning," and forced them to hold heavy buckets filled with water for long periods of time to "soften them up." Despite the thorough and relentless interrogations, no answers were uncovered concerning the lost blueprint. The engineers and blueprinters only weakly shook their heads in submission at the end of each grilling.

# 9
# The Mystery Solved

**Summer 1938**

The officers decided to change their strategy and further isolate the suspects. Each man was tried individually for espionage, an offense that carried the death penalty. The officers were certain that the crime had been committed by one man, and they tried to pressure the suspects into denouncing one of their colleagues. Not one of them, however, would name a guilty party in the incident. The detainees would return to their cells after questioning, their swollen faces dripping with blood.

The cells were unbearably hot. The only sensation was the pain of mosquitoes, lice, and bedbugs biting in the darkness. The prisoners were not permitted to take baths, and their bodies were permanently covered with sweat and dirt. The wounds they sustained during questioning were soon infected, and the pain kept them from sleeping.

While the loss of the blueprint was crucial and the arrest and questioning of the employees essential, the interrogations performed by the military police were desperate, inefficient, and extremely cruel. The men had never discussed their work with their friends and families since they had begun to work on the No. 2 Battleship project, and they wondered why they were suddenly being subjected to such painful and humiliating treatment.

After several weeks of intense grilling, the eight men were mentally and physically exhausted. A strange expression of fear and confusion appeared in their eyes each time they were pulled out of their cells. At this point they could only respond to police questioning with a silent quiver of terror.

Investigations at the shipyard were extended to the kitchens and even the toilets. The investigators pulled the panelling off the walls of some of the buildings, and the secret police even checked the backgrounds of employees in departments that had nothing to do with the battleship or the blueprint.

Two weeks passed. The sudden interruption in the flow of blueprints caused an enormous back-up in construction procedures. No one aside from the investigators and the heads of department knew that a top-secret document had been lost, and supervisors from the various divisions working on the ship would barge into the Design Department demanding blueprints.

Relations between the office workers and the investigating team were also becoming increasingly strained. The investigators were searching shipyard offices during working hours, scattering papers around in their frenzied search and creating complete chaos wherever they went.

The aftershock of the blueprint incident spread beyond Nagasaki, and the news soon made its way to the group of shipyard engineers who had been sent to the Kure. Rear Admiral Nobutsune Masaki of the arsenal's Shipbuilding Department was obliged to summon Takeji Kawara, the head of the Nagasaki design team, to his office to inform him of the situation.

"Do you realize that a very grave incident has occurred in Nagasaki?" the rear admiral asked grimly. "A top-secret military blueprint has been lost."

The blueprint in question was one that Kawara's group had copied from an original in Kure and sent to the shipyard.

"I don't suspect your group in the incident," the rear admiral said in a tone that seemed to belie his words. "The suspects are all members of the Design Department, and investigations are well under way. It seems they have been narrowed down to a few suspects."

Masaki questioned Kawara about how the design had been sent to Nagasaki and told him to be especially careful in future.

The engineer left the meeting troubled, wondering which of his colleagues the police had arrested as suspects in the case. The next day he learned that the room of one of his subordinates had been ransacked by a group of men calling themselves policemen. Other men in his group reported that police officers were asking questions about them in the neighborhood.

In the meantime the investigators at the shipyard were beginning to show signs of exhaustion. They had scoured every nook and cranny of the complex and thoroughly searched even the most unlikely areas. Sakakibara had become emaciated, with sunken cheeks and swollen eyes. Despite the fruitless investigation, he was still determined. One day he made an unlikely suggestion: "Should we try asking a clairvoyant to find the blueprint?"

He was a man who ordinarily did not believe in palmistry or any other irrational practices, but who nonetheless was in dire need of the answer to a mystery.

One of his engineers had heard of a clairvoyant in Sasebo, who was supposed to have a mysterious talent for finding lost objects. The man was reputed to have located important documents for the Kurume Regiment. The clairvoyant had told them to look in the library, and the documents had turned up when the building had been searched.

Sakakibara decided to send a subordinate to Sasebo to talk to the clairvoyant and bring him back to Nagasaki. When the man arrived at the shipyard, he already knew a blueprint had been lost. It only took a few minutes of meditation for him to come up with the approximate location of the document.

"You will find what you are looking for in a large room of a building thirty meters from the sea. It's inside a small closet," he said.

The only building in the shipyard thirty meters from the coast was the administration building. Sakakibara divided his men and had them search the closets of the Design Department, the General Affairs Department and the Sales Department. But all of these offices had already been thoroughly searched, and the blueprint was not found.

About one month after the blueprint had been lost, the secret police made the eight employees reenact the events of the day of the incident in a room at Nagasaki police headquarters.

Tables were arranged exactly as they were in the top-security room. There was even a mock-up of the caged blueprint storage area. One by one, each employee's memories were recorded, including their slightest recollections of the day's activities. As the reenactment progressed a slight discrepancy surfaced at a time corresponding to around four o'clock in the afternoon. Several of the employees vaguely remembered some suspicious actions by one of the two blueprinters.

The hour of 4:00 P.M. had a special meaning to the workers in the blueprint division. It was the time when the scrap paper used for their calculations was collected. In order to prevent this paper from being carelessly discarded or taken out of the top-security room, the engineers were provided with a scrap-paper pad with numbered sheets. When a draftsman finished with a sheet, he would rip it off the pad along with the one below it, just in case some of the figures might have passed through to the other sheet. Both sheets were thrown into the waste bin provided.

On the day of the incident the administrator had emerged from the storage cage and begun removing the used sheets of scrap paper from the bin, arranging them in numerical order. He then crammed the waste paper into a bag and ordered the two blueprinters carry it away. The three men left the room and carried the large sack of paper to the boiler room in the shipyard's generator plant. There they threw the waste paper into the furnace. The administrator waited until he was certain the paper had been completely incinerated.

The small discrepancy in the employees' accounts of the four o'clock ritual revolved around the actions of the nineteen-year-old blueprinter who had helped carry the bag to the incinerator. While the other employees said that he had returned to his desk for a moment before leaving the room, he insisted that he had not. Investigators had finally discovered a hole in an otherwise perfect cover-up.

They took the young blueprinter into a separate room and began to question him intensely about his actions in the late afternoon of the day of the incident. Sometime after dusk investigators lost their patience with the boy and threw him over the desk in the interrogation room. Between cries of pain, he confessed that he had taken the blueprint out of the top-security room.

With news of the blueprinter's confession, Sato and Hirata rushed to police headquarters. To these men, having identified the perpetrator of the crime was much less important than finding out to whom the boy had given the blueprint. But, according to the boy, the blueprint had already been burned in the incinerator.

"On the day of the incident, I carried the trash bag with the scrap paper in it back to my desk. Seeing the blueprint I had been working on lying in the open right-hand drawer of my desk, I made sure no one was watching and quickly shoved it into the trash bag. Then I followed the manager and the other blueprinter to the boiler room and threw the blueprint into the furnace with the other scrap paper," he confessed.

The boy's motives for stealing the blueprint were trivial: He simply wanted to be free from the restrictions of working in a top-security area and was hoping that his action might be a ticket out.

Raised in a middle-class family, he had joined the shipyard immediately after graduating from a vocational high school. His grades at school were good, and he was considered a hard worker. It was his good reputation that had caused him to be chosen as a blueprinter in the top-security room of the Design Department.

In the beginning he felt honored to have been selected to work there and was enthusiastic about the job, but as time passed he became more and more dissatisfied. The engineers working in the top-security room were some of the best in the shipyard, but the two blueprinters had no defined responsibilities and were forced to perform menial tasks as required.

While his peers at the shipyard were gaining valuable experience, the young blueprinter in the top-security room was forced to sweep the floor, fetch tea, and take out the trash. Taking the trash out to the boiler room, like a common janitor, especially hurt the boy's self-respect. The engineers were all over thirty, and the other blueprinter was almost ten years older and so serious about his work that he barely talked to his younger colleague.

The boy soon felt that he could no longer bear his assignment. Other shipyard workers had dubbed the room "the prison" or the "bird cage" because of the storage area. The longer the boy spent in the sunless top-security room, the stronger his urge to escape to a place where he would have more freedom. All he had to do, he thought, was make one major mistake, and he would be transferred to a different job. That day he had grabbed the blueprint on his desk on impulse, without looking at the information it contained, shoved it into his trash bag, and thrown it into the furnace.

The loss of the blueprint had caused a much more serious crisis in the shipyard than the boy had ever imagined. He was frightened when he saw how flustered the administrator had become when he realized the blueprint was lost. When the Navy men had shown up a few minutes later with crazed looks on their faces, he was horrified. He did not know what the repercussions would be if he were discovered, so he decided to keep quiet about the blueprint no matter what happened.

The investigators suspected the engineers more than they did the blueprinters, and, as the youngest of the group, he had escaped the brunt of the questioning. He was only asked from time to time about the particulars of the work area and his colleagues. Nevertheless, he did not believe he could hide his guilt forever and during the month-long interrogation he had struggled with his conscience.

Captain Hirata did not believe the boy's confession at first. He thought he might be saying he had burned the blueprint to hide the fact that he had given it to a foreign agent. He instructed the secret police to continue their questioning, but the additional information only supported the boy's original story.

The boy had few acquaintances outside his family, and he went straight home after finishing work. About a month before the incident he had suddenly become very quiet, and he often complained to his parents that he wanted to be transferred to a different division.

Hirata gradually began to believe the boy's story. Considering the design of the top-security room, the only possible way a blueprint could be taken out without anyone's knowledge was with the trash. The motive, too, was typically trivial for a youth of the blueprinter's age.

"We have no doubt the kid is telling the truth," the police interrogators confidently told Hirata and Sato; both men responded with an obvious sigh of relief.

The six engineers and the other blueprinter were released from police custody after the boy's confession. Severely weakened by the ordeal, they returned home bruised and emaciated. The boy was tried and sentenced to three years imprisonment with two years probation. He was led quietly away to Miike, where he was put on a boat bound for Manchuria. His family subsequently left Nagasaki.

Of the seven shipyard employees released from police custody after the incident, three suffered nervous breakdowns and were unable to return to work for an extended period of time. When they finally went back to shipyard, they refused to be reassigned to the Design Department.

# 10
# Red Chalk and Loose Lips

**Autumn 1938**

Autumn came early that year. At the beginning of October the Okunchi Festival filled the streets of Nagasaki with the sounds of flutes and drums.

The mood at the shipyard was in a sharp contrast to the festive spirit of the city. Memories of the blueprint debacle hung like a pall in the air. Stories about the eight arrested employees passed among shipyard workers. The incident served as a sobering reminder of the risks they were taking by working on a top-secret military project. Workers who had taken the oath of secrecy were proud to have been selected, yet they also felt they had been thrown into a security cage for the duration of the project.

New engineers and blueprinters had been assigned to the top-security room in the Design Department, and though the steady flow of blueprints resumed, work on the battleship was showing signs of lagging behind schedule. Watanabe paced nervously between the slipway and his office.

The blueprint incident was the major reason for the two-month delay, but the project was also being slowed by a shortage of men at the shipyard. In previous years the yard had always received a good response to recruitment drives, but the number of applicants had fallen dramatically that year, and many workers were quitting to find jobs in smaller factories.

This trend did not affect the more experienced skilled workers, but many new recruits were leaving. In order to make up for the shortage of applicants, the shipyard sent scouts to remote areas of

Kyushu to hire new workers. Despite the exodus from the other divisions, the staffing levels on the No. 2 Battleship project remained unchanged.

The work that had been most delayed was the expansion and reinforcement of the No. 2 slipway. Although this had begun immediately after the launch of the *Chikuma*, and should have been completed within three months, seven months had already gone by. The reinforcement of the aft portion of the slipway—the section that would take the whole weight of the ship during the launch —had been postponed drastically. The hardest thing about the job was that the area was partially flooded at high tide. The workers had to take off their clothes and jump into the waist-high water in order to bolt together the steel girders needed to reinforce the slipway. This was not a major problem in the summer, but when autumn came, and the water suddenly cooled, the work became a painful chore.

Fires were strictly forbidden on the slipway because of the danger of igniting the hemp blinds. The workers would rub one another's legs with straw ropes, hoping that friction would create enough heat for them to recover from the chill before going back into the water. Rainy days and night shifts were especially difficult. With their teeth chattering and bodies shaking, workers continually pushed themselves to the limits of endurance. More and more sustained physical injuries because of the cold, and other employees had to be brought in to replace them.

Because of the delay in reinforcing the slipway, workers were forced to concentrate on the battleship's central portion. Rising from the double layer of steel plates on the bottom of the ship, the transverse ribs looked like the skeleton of a giant dinosaur. As work began on the sides of the hull, steel plates were riveted onto the outside of the ribs, which had already reached a height of almost fifteen meters. Inside the screens, the deafening sound of rivets being driven into steel and the glow of blue welding sparks filled the air.

Kajiwara was ruthlessly strict about riveting standards. When he came to inspect that day's work, he would carry a stick of red chalk with which he would mark an **X** on even the slightest flaw in a rivet that had already been driven into the steel. The engineers and workers would exchange looks of exasperation whenever Kajiwara approached with his stick of red chalk.

Two highly-experienced workers were in charge of driving the rivets into the steel plates with enormous riveting guns. They were well aware that a badly driven rivet would cause leaks once the vessel was afloat, and that construction mistakes could have disastrous consequences if the ship were hit by an enemy shell or torpedo. They had more than enough confidence in the quality of their work, and they considered Kajiwara's inspections to be humiliating and cruel.

On one inspection Kajiwara turned to look at the workers as they bit their lips in self-restraint. "We will not use anything on this battleship that is imperfect," he shouted. "Everything must be flawless. Change all of these rivets immediately!"

He quickly walked away, leaving the riveters in a fury. They had been ordered to re-drive the rivets, but "faulty" rivets that had already been driven into the hard steel plates were not easy to remove. They would either have to be heated to widen the holes, or pulled out by brute force. The re-driving work would take the entire night.

By mid-November the work reinforcing the aft portion of the slipway had finally been completed. Two thousand tons of I-shaped steel girders had been used in the process. Workers could finally begin construction on the twenty-meter-long, eight-meter-high, ninety-one-ton stern area. The gantry cranes slowly hoisted the heavy stern materials, including the steel plates that would be used to protect the ship's rudders, over the empty hull. The materials were laid in a huge pile at the far end of the slipway.

On December 30, 1938, Tamai and Watanabe made their annual progress report to Captain Hirata. By the close of 1938 the materials used so far on the No. 2 slipway weighed 6,800 tons, and were held together by 589,097 rivets. The number of workers on the project had increased to 2,164. The ship's launch weight had been estimated at 36,000 tons, so the current weight meant that less than twenty percent of the ship had been completed.

Hirata looked at the report with a dissatisfied expression. "Construction on the No.1 Battleship at Kure is proceeding ahead of schedule," he said. "The international situation is deteriorating. I cannot permit construction on this ship to be delayed. You must try to make up for this time lag after the New Year."

Tamai and Watanabe left the naval supervisor's office having spoken very few words. The New Year's holiday lasted until January 3, and work resumed on January 4. Watanabe called his subordinates into his office and urged them to catch up on the time they had lost over the previous year.

* * *

That year the Japanese Army in China captured Canton and Hanchow. In response, Britain and the United States stepped up their aid to the Chinese Nationalists. Clashes between Japanese and Soviet forces on the Manchurian border showed signs of turning into a full-scale war. In Europe, Hitler ordered the invasion of western Czechoslovakia as the first step in his plan to conquer the entire European continent. It was not yet certain whether Japan would get involved in a European conflict, but if a large-scale war did erupt, it was only natural that the Navy would ask the shipyard to push forward the completion date for the No. 2 Battleship.

Watanabe was plagued with increasing pressure and anxiety. He would frequently visit Kure on his way to the Bureau of Naval Construction in Tokyo. Construction of the No. 1 Battleship was proceeding smoothly, in contrast to work on the No. 2 Battleship that was substantially behind schedule.

The workers on the No. 2 slipway were no longer permitted to take Sundays off, and those arriving for work at 8:00 A.M. stayed on the job until 9:30 P.M., while the second shift stayed regularly until 11:30 P.M. They were only given two days off a month, when the shipyard shut down its power plant.

Watanabe and Koga began making the rounds of the different divisions of the shipyard, where parts of the battleship were being manufactured or assembled, to encourage workers to work harder and faster.

In February an incident painfully reminiscent of the previous summer's blueprint crisis occurred at the No. 2 slipway. The culprit was again a young worker, who had stolen away from his coworkers during a break, measured the distance between the steel support columns of the gantry cranes, and computed the length of the slipway. On his way home from work that evening he stopped at a bar and had a few drinks. Before long he was telling the other customers about his calculations of the length of the battleship.

The worker was arrested by the secret police the next morning on his way to work. Tamai hung his head for a few moments when he heard the news. If the police decided to search the shipyard during their investigations, work on the battleship would be delayed once again, because the arrested man worked on the slipway itself.

Watanabe and Tamai immediately went to see Captain Hirata to explain the effects an investigation would have on the construction schedule.

Hirata remained silent as he listened to the two men's case. "I've got the picture," he said. "Leave this to me. However, I would like you to educate your employees a little better. Make sure this never happens again."

For Hirata, the prompt completion of the battleship was now the top priority. No one was really sure how he dealt with the matter, but the police never came to the shipyard, and the young worker was never seen again.

By February 1939 over 2,500 employees had taken the oath of secrecy and were working on the battleship project. Although it was inevitable that one or two would violate the oath, the Navy was too concerned with the effects of such a leak to allow one to occur. Watanabe called a meeting of all the shipyard managers and ordered them to review the contents of the oath with their employees.

In March workers began laying tubing for the electrical wiring in the bottom of the ship's hold near the stern. They installed eight 600-kilowatt generators in the hull to create 4,800 kilowatts of electrical power on board—the amount of energy then supplied to a city of 30,000 people. This enormous amount of current was needed to operate the ship's main and auxiliary guns, anti-aircraft guns, and machine guns, as well as the automatic ammunition loading for the main guns, the helm, and the emergency pumping system.

The electricity was distributed via eight separate cables that branched off into the innumerable compartments of the vessel. As the cables approached their various branch terminals, they became so numerous that it was almost impossible for the electrical engineers to sort them out. They needed a blueprint of the entire battleship to distribute the wires, but the shipyard would not send such a design to the construction area because it was a top military secret. Thus the complicated process of wiring the battleship was also carried out by referring to a series of smaller blueprints and pasting them together to figure out the larger picture.

# 11
# A Flash in the Dark

**Spring 1939**

One night in early April Watanabe, Koga, and Kajiwara dressed in plain clothes so as not to attract attention and went to the Oura beach directly opposite the shipyard. In the darkness in front of them loomed the slipways of the Nagasaki Shipyard. The hemp screens hanging across the No. 2 slipway and the neighboring No. 1 slipway, where most of the materials for the battleship were stored, stuck out noticeably from the rest of the shipyard.

The three men were looking at the No. 2 slipway when Kajiwara whispered urgently, "I saw another flash."

The No. 2 slipway would light up for a split second in the darkness. There was a constant glow within the hemp screens from the overhead lights used for the evening shift, but occasionally a brief flash from the welding guns would illuminate the inside of the construction area.

Watanabe and the others stared glumly at the scene across the harbor. The United States and British consulates were just behind them.

"There's another flash," Koga said.

This latest flash shone at a different angle from the previous one.

"This is no good," Watanabe whispered sullenly.

One of the shipyard engineers had reported that the light of the welding guns could be seen from the Oura coast road, which he took on his way home from the plant. If a spy set up a camera on the beach at night and took exposures when the light flashes exploded from the welding guns, he would be able to see a limited portion of the interior of the slipway. By calculating the distance between the camera and the slipway, he could easily determine the scale of the battleship under construction. Worst of all, the United States and British consulates had the best view of the shipbuilding area.

After discussing the problem with his colleagues, Watanabe decided that their only recourse was to thicken the hemp screens on the coastal side of the slipway. In order to be absolutely certain that the new screening method would be effective, Koga took photographs of the flashes produced by the welding guns from the Oura beach, not just at night but also during the day, to see if enough light seeped through the screens to produce a photograph.

Shortly after noon on the following day Koga and Watanabe took four welders from the No. 2 slipway to a remote area of the shipyard and had them work their welding guns behind hemp screens to see how much light would show through. Watanabe and his assistant took photographs at 100-meter increments. Starting at a distance of 100 meters, they worked their way to 700 meters, and then repeated the process with a double and triple layer of screens. The experiment was repeated again that night.

The results on the processed film were just as Koga had expected. During the day almost none of the light from the welding guns was visible, but at night the flashes of light showed up distinctly when only one hemp screen was used. With two screens, almost no light leaked through, and photographs taken at distances greater than 200 meters were almost completely blank.

"It's a good thing we noticed the problem so early," Watanabe said to Kajiwara as they were looking at the photographs.

The shape of the vessel under construction was still not recognizable, and even if spies had been taking photographs of the ship, they probably would not be able to estimate its size from the portion that had been completed so far. Watanabe immediately ordered workers to start adding hemp screens around the ship, and the work area grew increasingly dark.

"The consulates and foreign residences still worry me," Kaji-wara said after the additional hemp screens had been hung.

He was gazing out over the harbor toward the Oura coast where the United States and the British consulates stood side by side. On the slope behind them was the Nagasaki branch of the Hong Kong-Shanghai Bank and the residence of a British bank employee by the name of Harris. Even further up the slope was the Glover Estate.

"We're all right now. The problem will be after the ship is launched," Kajiwara said, his eyebrows knitted tensely. "Once we hook the ship to the outfitting dock, it will be in the open."

Almost immediately after Kajiwara had noticed the problem, however, a solution came from Nagasaki City Hall. The Hong Kong-Shanghai Bank was soon to close its Nagasaki branch, and the bank building and Harris residence would be put up for sale. When he heard the news Captain Hirata worried that the buildings might be bought by another foreign company.

He immediately contacted the Bureau of Naval Construction, which decided that the Sasebo Naval Station would buy the two buildings. The Umegasaki Police Station was moved into the former bank building, and the Harris residence was designated as a clubhouse for Navy personnel visiting Nagasaki.

The Navy and shipyard were relieved. Two of the buildings that worried them most had been filled with police and Navy personnel, and could now act as a base to strengthen security along the coast. Immediately after they had bought the bank, the shipyard and Navy began talking about buying the Glover Estate.

The Glover Estate was built by an Englishman called Thomas Brooke Glover, who had arrived in Nagasaki in 1860. From the last days of the shogunate into the Meiji period, Glover had made a fortune by selling guns to clans loyal to the emperor. After a lucrative career as an arms dealer, he started a firm importing machinery to Japan.

In the late 1930s an elderly man by the name of Tomisaburo Glover was quietly spending his last days there. He was Glover's son by his Japanese wife. There were many rooms left unused in the spacious mansion, and the shipyard thought that even if they could not purchase the whole estate, it could at least rent out a portion of the building.

The shipyard made a request to Glover through Nagasaki City Hall, and the old man responded that he would be interested in any reasonable offer, if they deemed the purchase necessary. The General Affairs Department of the shipyard sent a representative to work out the details of the purchase, and in the end managed to buy the whole building.

Glover moved to a small servants' cottage at back of the main house. The shipyard designated the Glover Mansion a club for shipyard employees, but this was merely a front. The building was closed, and a small part of it was used as a station for the military police who patrolled the hills.

The only remaining foreign-owned buildings with a good view of the shipyard were the United States and British consulates. But even the Navy, with all of its power, could do nothing to move these buildings, and the military police was forced to station a large number of officers in the area of the two consulates.

\* \* \*

At the end of April Prince Kuni of the Naval General Staff visited Nagasaki to inspect the progress on the No. 2 Battleship. Tamai was able to report that although less than thirty percent of the pre-launch construction work had been completed, the shipyard had caught up with the original timetable for the project. He added that about 1,000 employees were now working on the No. 2 slipway itself, while about another 700 were working on the ship in other divisions of the yard. Several hundred more were involved in design, planning, and related tasks. The atmosphere in Watanabe's office was considerably brighter than a few months earlier.

On the slipway, 11,000 tons of steel, requiring 1.41 million rivets, had been assembled. The hull towered higher and higher above the slipway floor, and the munitions chambers had been attached at the bow and stern. One section of the boiler rooms was also under construction. Twelve boilers would send steam to the engines to rotate the screw propellers. The boiler rooms, because of their function as the very source of propulsion for the battleship, were protected by thick steel plates, just like the engine room. Each boiler was 8.3 meters high and covered an area of sixty-six square meters. These were placed in the center of the battleship in three rows of four across.

On July 1 a ceremony was held to mark the start of construction of the *Kashino* on the No. 3 slipway. This 10,360-ton freighter was being built specifically to ferry parts for the No. 2 Battleship from Kure to Nagasaki, and the Navy had planned for its construction at the same time it was designing the No. 2 Battleship.

Among the parts to be produced at Kure and then shipped to Nagasaki were the battleship's nine forty-six-centimeter guns. Due to their enormous size and weight, overland transportation was out of the question, and the only alternative was to transport them by sea. An ordinary cargo ship with a hold large enough to carry the guns, however, would probably sink under their immense weight. Therefore the Bureau of Naval Construction had planned a specially designed vessel to carry the guns.

At that time important personnel changes were taking place in the shipyard's Design Department. The design director of the No. 2 Battleship project, Naosaburo Izumiyama, was transferred to Tokyo and replaced by Itsuo Matsushita. One of his new responsibilities was to supervise the design and building of the *Kashino*.

Watanabe had assigned the design of the *Kashino* to Korekazu Kawakita. When the engineer first saw the plans for the new ship, he blinked in disbelief at its odd shape. The vessel's mid-section was strangely widened, and the deck had a hole 15.7 meters by14.8 meters. Studying the designs in more detail, Kawakita realized the hole had been designed to accommodate one of the gun turrets of the No. 2 Battleship. The guns were to be attached directly into the *Kashino*. The unusual design of the freighter required certain alterations during construction. The most important point was stability. Unladen, the *Kashino* would float unusually high in the water and could easily capsize.

Matsushita helped Kawakita research ways to stabilize the ship, and the two engineers finally came up with the idea of pouring a mixture of cement and steel scrap into the bottom of the hull to act as ballast. The engineers decided to use steel scrap instead of gravel because it produced more weight at a lower volume. Workers at the No. 4 slipway labored on the strangely-shaped vessel at a furious pace, as if they were trying to catch up with the battleship being constructed on the neighboring slipway.

On August 23 the shipyard held its first flood test of the No. 2 Battleship's boiler system. This consisted of pouring a large quantity of water into the boiler rooms to see if the walls could withstand the pressure. During a battle it was vital that the walls of the boilers did not break if the hull was flooded. Workers at the No. 2 slipway began pumping water into the boiler rooms at 4:50 A.M.

Carefully measuring the strain produced on the steel walls by loosening the support girders at the four corners of each boiler room, they filled them to their full capacity. Measuring the water pressure on the walls, they discovered that 550 tons of water expanded the walls by about five millimeters. They then removed the water and emptied the boilers. The results of the test were satisfactory.

Small scale water-pressure tests had been started almost six months before on individual parts of the boilers. The tests were conducted on flood-control partitions, the sump tank, and the crude oil tanks. Altogether more than 300 parts of the boiler system had been tested for their resistance to water pressure.

By late August construction on the hull of the No. 2 Battleship had approached the halfway point, with 17,000 tons of material assembled on the slipway and 2.7 million rivets driven into the hull.

# 12
# Bad Dreams

**Autumn 1939**

On September 1, 1939, the German Army invaded Poland. Three days later England and France declared war on Germany. The atmosphere at the shipyard was tense. The Japanese government stated that it would not become involved in the European conflict, declaring that it would strive instead for a quick solution to the China Incident.

After signing alliances with Germany and Italy, however, it was unlikely that Japan could remain a neutral third party for long. Relations with the Soviet Union deteriorated further in July, and the United States and Britain continued to step up their economic pressure on Japan.

Workers at the shipyard became accustomed to the feverish pace of work, which steadily increased as summer ended and fall approached. The electrical generators and the air-conditioning system were installed on the battleship.

At the end of October work began on a 430-ton, 1,600 horsepower tugboat called the *Sakufu-maru*. This vessel, like the *Kashino*, had a direct relationship to the No. 2 Battleship project. The shipyard had no tugboats capable of towing the battleship's huge hull after the launch, so a special tugboat had to be built.

One day, as the lower half of the No. 2 Battleship hull finally began taking shape, Koga entered the director's office to find Watanabe looking over some documents.

"Looking at it taking shape on the slipway, it seems like this battleship could never be sunk," Koga remarked proudly.

Watanabe raised his head and smiled at his assistant. As Koga's remark indicated, the separate sections of the ship, including the munitions chambers, the engine room, the boiler rooms, the generator rooms, the transformer room, the bridge, the communications room, and the pumping room, were all surrounded by thick steel plates. Each of these sections resembled a self-contained vessel.

Koga continued enthusiastically, "I heard from the Navy that the forty-six-centimeter guns on the No. 1 and No. 2 battleships have a maximum range of 41,400 meters. That means they can hit targets over the horizon. The shells weigh a ton and a half each. I've never heard of that kind of firepower on a ship before."

The armor plating on the ship's hull was equally impressive. When it had first started making plans for this new class of battleship, the Bureau of Naval Construction estimated that the enemy's largest guns would have a maximum diameter of forty centimeters, and the armor plating on the battleships was planned to withstand the impact of a shell fired from such guns. Later the Navy decided that the U.S. would build ships equipped with forty-six-centimeter guns and adjusted the thickness of the armor plating accordingly.

"I understand why we're using those incredible forty-centimeter-thick steel plates on the sides of the hull," Koga said, "but even the plates below the waterline are ridiculously thick. No one is saying anything about it, but the men on the slipway are surprised that we're armoring the bottom of the ship so heavily."

Koga looked at his superior inquisitively. Normally, the steel plating below the waterline would not be noticeably thicker than the rest of the hull, but the plating on the No. 2 Battleship was twenty centimeters thick. On top of the plate, a convex fortification, called a bulge, had been constructed over the entire hull.

"That's an important feature of the design of the new battleships. Thick armor plating below the waterline is unheard of in foreign warships, but the design is based on the results of the test firings done on the hull of the *Tosa*," Watanabe said.

He went on to explain that the Navy's experiments disproved the traditional belief that shells hitting the water immediately lost their direction and speed, and so could do little damage. The *Tosa* had shown that when guns were aimed at the submerged portion of the hull, the shells traveled through the water and penetrated the torpedo shielding, causing substantial damage.

The Navy had learned that it could not ignore the destructive power of a shell after it entered the water. To further reap the benefits of this discovery, Navy engineers had developed shells designed to travel underwater and pierce the submerged portions of enemy ships. This research had yielded an exclusive secret weapon for Japan: the type 91 hull-piercing shell.

The new shell retained its original shape as it traveled through the air, but once it penetrated the water, it shed its cap to reveal a tip designed specifically to travel underwater. The shell did not veer sideways when it hit the water but continued on a straight trajectory with a minimal drop in velocity. The release of the shell casing when it made contact with the water also left the head buoyant and kept it near the surface, allowing the shell to impact on the ship's hull at its most vulnerable point.

The Navy predicted that such underwater shells would also be developed abroad, and they began strengthening the underwater defenses on the hulls of their ships. They started equipping all their new ships with special defenses, and had planned even more elaborate underwater armor for the No. 1 and No. 2 battleships.

When he heard this explanation, Koga smiled and said, "So the *Tosa* wasn't sunk in vain."

Watanabe lit a cigarette and said, "The Navy must have put a lot of thought into this design."

Koga laughed. "The workers at the No. 2 slipway are completely bewildered by all these defenses. There are so many of them that they waste most of their time wandering around the bottom of the ship's hull, looking for which sections are supposed to get the special defense plating."

There were 1,147 watertight compartments in the new vessel,

and almost 700 of these had been equipped with special defenses. The munitions chambers and other fortified compartments were surrounded by thick steel plates, but if the entire hull of the ship was armored in this way, the weight of the ship would be enormous. Armor was not used in less vital areas, where a special type of honeycombed steel plate was used instead. If the hull was damaged in these areas, the flooding would be stopped by the network of watertight compartments inside.

Koga, engrossed by Watanabe's explanation, lowered himself into a chair. "What about welding? That incident in the Fourth Squadron is really limiting us, isn't it?" he said.

As an engineer, he thought that the construction of the No. 2 Battleship should involve more welding, which would result in a much lighter ship than the riveting method they were currently using. But very little welding was being used on either the No.1 or No. 2 battleships.

"That's right," Watanabe said, "minimal welding."

During naval exercises in September 1935 the fleet had been divided into a red team and a blue team. The Fourth Squadron of the red team had encountered a typhoon with fifty-meter-per-second winds on the way to the Sanriku Shallows from the Tsugaru Strait.

The squadron's commander, thinking that the storm would a good opportunity to test his ships for their ability to handle rough seas, ordered his command into the typhoon. The continuous onslaught of violent waves caused a series of unexpected structural failures: Bridges were blown off main decks, and the hull of the destroyer *Hatsuyuki* split in two just forward of its bridge. The ships that sustained the worst damage were not ones that had been welded, but later tests showed that with less riveting and more welding, the damage would have been even greater. The Navy was alarmed by the incident and decided that vital structural areas of the hull had to be riveted.

"I heard the Navy is planning a No. 3 Battleship," Koga remarked hesitantly.

"Who did you hear that from?" Watanabe asked, stunned. He was trying to hide his surprise from his subordinate, but the fear on his face told Koga that he had mentioned a subject he should know nothing about.

Koga looked back at his superior blankly. "I heard it from the Bureau of Naval Construction," he said.

The tension eased from Watanabe's face. "Oh, so you know too," he said. "The Navy has already decided to start construction on the No. 3 Battleship at the Yokosuka Arsenal and of the No. 4 Battleship at the Kure Arsenal."

"A No. 4 Battleship?" Koga said.

"That's right," Watanabe said, "four 70,000-ton battleships. The Navy has made big plans. But remember, this is completely confidential," Watanabe added with a slightly irritated tone in his voice.

Koga simply nodded.

* * *

In mid-November Captain Hirata was replaced as chief supervisor of naval construction by Commander Mantaro Shimamoto. At just about the same time Rear Admiral Keiji Fukuda of the Bureau of Naval Construction came to observe the construction of the battleship in Nagasaki. As the person in charge of basic planning for both the No. 1 and No. 2 battleships, Fukuda seemed to take a deep personal satisfaction at the sight of the construction under way on the slipway. Almost 2,000 engineers and workers were gathered like a swarm of ants around the enormous steel structure, while overhead cranes swung the larger pieces into position. Completely enthralled by the scene before him, Fukuda walked from one vantage point to another, taking a long, intent look at the construction process.

"It's progressing much faster than I expected. When are you planning to launch?" he asked Watanabe when they had returned to his office.

"In about a year," Watanabe answered confidently.

"I'm sure you have confidence in your work, but we're keeping a close eye on you to see how smoothly the project progresses. It could easily be considered the most difficult assignment in shipbuilding history," Fukuda said. He nodded sympathetically at Watanabe, to show he understood the pressure he was under as project director.

The stress, in fact, was affecting Watanabe even when he slept. He was afflicted with a recurring nightmare in which he was attending the launch of the No. 2 Battleship. The enormous hull of the battleship would begin to slide off the slipway, when suddenly a shrill splitting noise would erupt, and a wide fracture would appear in the slipway's concrete floor. The concrete would surge up with amazing force. Watanabe would scream, and the hull, picking up speed, would begin listing to port. The angle of the list would increase until objects began falling from the deck with a loud crash.

As the workers on the slipway became aware of the falling objects, they would begin to scatter out of the ship's path. A crashing sound filled the air as the ship capsized on the slipway. Dust and debris sprayed upwards, spewing high into the air. With the crashing sound of the hull, Watanabe also heard another stranger noise—as if wet cloth had been suddenly wrung dry: Hundreds of human bodies were being crushed under the battleship. A crimson liquid welled up from the hull and trickled down the concrete slipway, turning the sea red.

The screams of the injured filled Watanabe's ears, and he would run around in circles, screaming hysterically. Sometimes Watanabe would be awakened by his own screams, sometimes his wife would wake him up. He was always drenched in a cold sweat. Then he would lie with his eyes open, unable to sleep until dawn. The nightmares were so real that he could not shake off the fear they induced.

The vessel that now filled the No. 2 slipway was so huge that it was no longer possible to see in its entirety from any vantage point.

Watanabe could not begin to imagine how such a gigantic structure would slide smoothly off the No. 2 slipway into Nagasaki Harbor.

# 13

# Final Preparations

**Winter 1940**

Watanabe had been putting all of his efforts into the preparations for the moment the enormous hull of the No. 2 Battleship would be launched. His work slowly produced concrete results, but he was plagued by anxiety when shipbuilding experts like Rear Admiral Fukuda called the project the most difficult in shipbuilding history.

The zeal of the two engineers in charge of researching the ship's launch—Takeshi Hamada and Joshichi Omiya—helped put Watanabe's mind at ease. The two men had studied the launch records of large vessels worldwide. Starting with the 70,000-ton *Queen Mary* in England, they analyzed the launches of 233 vessels.

Even with all of this data they had few hints on how to proceed with the launch of the No. 2 Battleship because of the topography of Nagasaki Harbor. Their first reaction was that they had been set an impossible task. But the young and scholarly Hamada traded knowledge and ideas with Omiya, a seasoned launch veteran, and they trudged their way through unknown territory. According to their calculations, the launch weight of the ship would be slightly less than 36,000 tons, and the pressure on the slipway would be 19.3 tons per square meter. They calculated that a three-percent gradient would be a sufficient slope for the ship's hull to slide off the slipway.

Watanabe ordered Omiya to start assembling the launch platform that he and Hamada had designed on paper. Even for an experienced engineer like Omiya, many of the details of this launch were unfamiliar. The first challenge was the construction of the four-meter launch platform itself. Sturdy pine would be needed to construct a platform that could support the enormous weight of the hull as it slid off the slipway. In order to build a platform four meters wide, Omiya would have to use nine forty-four-centimeter-thick rectangular pieces of Douglas fir placed side by side and held together by steel bolts.

The entire weight of the battleship would rest on the launch platform, so if the pine split, the ship's hull would capsize on the slipway. To guard against this, Omiya decided to use unusually thick steel bolts, which he thought would not to bend or break under any circumstances. He had five-and-a-half-centimeter bolts forged, but a problem arose immediately, because the shipyard had no drills large enough to bore the outsized holes for the bolts. Omiya made a special request to the tool shop and had it forge several types of experimental drill bits.

However, the real problem in constructing the platform started after a suitable drill had been made. Omiya did not realize how difficult it would be to drill such a large hole in a four-meter pine stack. He thought it might be difficult, but that if he assigned a veteran driller to the job, it would be finished in a few days. His hopes were shattered when the first driller found that the pine warped in its softer sections, and the drill would not drive straight. The frustrated driller obediently persisted day after day, but still had no luck after ten days of careful work.

Thinking over the problem, Omiya thought that a task which proved too difficult for a veteran might be best left to a complete beginner. He selected about ten young workers who seemed to have some determination.

He assembled his novices and told them what he had in mind, "This drilling is vital to the success of the launch. I want you to all empty your minds when you do this job. Do you understand? I don't want you to think like drillers at all."

Omiya taught the men how to use the drills, cautioned them on the dangers and had them try their hand at drilling some holes. The drills, however, emerged far from the prescribed marks on the other side of the pine stacks.

Omiya was furious with himself for using such simplistic logic. If the job was impossible for an experienced driller, it would be doubly impossible for a beginner. Despite the setback, he was determined not to give in.

"Just put a little work into it. There's nothing you can't do if you don't try," Omiya would say, trying to encourage the frustrated young workers.

The drillers spent days simply trying to drill a straight hole through the four meters of pine. The pieces of wood they were using soon became riddled with holes, and new test material was continuously brought for the workers. Some of the drillers began to get tired of the pointless work and asked to be moved to other jobs. Omiya would grant these men their transfers without hesitation, but with a very strong reprimand.

"All right, I'll transfer you. We don't need men like you around here anyway."

Many of the young drillers' hands were stained with blood, and thick calluses developed on their palms from the continuous drilling. Nevertheless, the drills would always veer off on a tangent half way through the stack. After each failure they would limply hang their heads in resignation for a few minutes. The more they failed, the more careless they became—at times their attempts were completely haphazard. Omiya would notice when the men were getting careless and try to get them back on track.

"Even our veterans couldn't do this job properly. You are beginners. If you can pull this off, you'll be experienced drillers. If you don't feel like doing this job any more, go to another section. I only want the ones who want to become experts at what they do."

After the first year more than half of the drillers still remained on the job. After about eighteen months they managed on rare occasions to bore a straight hole through the wood. After two years all of the drillers were able to produce a straight hole one hundred percent of the time.

Twenty-four months after initial drilling had started, Omiya stood on the opposite side of a four-meter pine stack from the drillers, staring at the small circles on the surface marking the point where the drills were supposed to emerge. To his amazement, each of the rotating heads jumped one by one from the center of the targets on his side of the stack. His band of beginners had succeeded. Omiya silently congratulated himself for having won such a risky gamble.

The next problem Omiya was faced with was the choice of tallow to be used as a lubricant for the launch structure. The launch structure consisted of a fixed platform under a sliding platform. Some kind of lubricant had to be laid between the two platforms, but the tallow to be used for the launch of the No. 2 Battleship had to meet certain specifications. Because the battleship was much heavier than anything ever launched at the shipyard, the lubricant had to be able to withstand the pressure and friction produced by the enormous weight of the hull.

The launch platform on the No. 2 slipway had to be built comparatively early, and Omiya needed a solid animal fat that would not harden or deteriorate before it was time for the launch. After testing tallows from several of the shipyard's suppliers, Omiya decided to use the one produced by an oil and fat manufacturer in Osaka called Okada.

As he proceeded with experiments on the tallow, Omiya invited the president of the company, Kumajiro Okada, to visit the shipyard to observe the testing. In order for Okada to visit the test site, however, he would have to walk through a corridor with a clear view of the No. 2 Battleship. Omiya had the passageway enclosed in aluminum plates so that the tallow supplier could not see into the No. 2 slipway.

Okada was curious about the strange tunnel. "Why do we have

to go through these tunnels like this, like a couple of moles?" he asked as he stooped through the aluminum-lined tunnel.

\* \* \*

The New Year's holidays in January 1940 were shorter than in previous years, and all of the workers at the shipyard returned to their jobs on January 3.

Construction of the six engine blocks was now completed, and the materials being assembled on the slipway for the vessel's bow and stern towered above the concrete floor. About seventy percent of the pre-launch work on the battleship had been finished.

At the end of February Tamai was promoted to the post of managing director of Mitsubishi head office in Tokyo, and Yoshiki Ogawa became the twelfth president of Nagasaki Shipyard. Watanabe was made vice president, while retaining his post of director of the No. 2 Battleship Construction Office. Kikuhei Shimizu replaced outgoing Vice President Inagaki, and the head of the Design Department, Etsushi Sakakibara was also promoted to the rank of vice president.

Ogawa had spent his career designing and building warships, and Shimizu was world famous as the designer of the MS engine. Mitsubishi figured that these two men, with the support of Watanabe and Sakakibara, would make the ideal management team for the battleship project.

Upon assuming his new post Ogawa immediately started to work with Watanabe trying to sort out the details of the launch. Watanabe had already set the launch date for November 1, 1940. They had eight months to make sure they had everything right.

Ogawa looked nervously at Watanabe when he announced the day of the launch. "You're sure that the tidal conditions and the weather predictions for that date are all right?" he asked.

The shipyard needed a high tide in order to launch the battleship. The tides were recorded every day by the Nagasaki Weather

Station, but these were figures for the tides outside the harbor. To use these tidal patterns to judge conditions inside the harbor would be inaccurate. The shipyard had installed its own equipment in the harbor beside the slipway three years before, and according to calculations based on their own data, the tide would be at its highest on November 1 at 8:55 A.M.

Watanabe's team had taken averages for temperature and weather conditions for the past three years and predicted that November 1 would provide ideal conditions.

"We have begun preparing the outfitting dock, so we can launch at any time in the near future," Watanabe explained, pointing at a map of the harbor.

After the launch the No. 2 Battleship would be hooked up to an outfitting dock near the slipway, where the main guns, the bridge, the smokestack, and other parts would be fitted. An ordinary dock, however, would not suffice for the No. 2 Battleship. The shipyard decided to cut into the mountain on the Mukaijima side and build a new outfitting dock of sufficient size. 160,000 cubic meters of soil were excavated from the harbor floor to give the dock a depth of eleven meters. The preparatory work on the outfitting dock had been finished two months before Watanabe had his meeting with Ogawa, but the problem remained of how to transfer the battleship's main guns from the cargo ship to the No. 2 Battleship. The largest crane ship in the shipyard had a hoisting capacity of 150 tons. This could be used to lift the auxiliary guns, but not the main ones.

"I have discussed this problem many times with the Navy," Watanabe said, "and we can borrow a crane ship with a 350-ton hoist capacity from the Sasebo Naval Station."

"Well, then the only problem left is whether or not you can finish construction on the ship's hull in time for November 1," Ogawa said.

Construction was proceeding according to schedule. It had only been two years since the initial assembly work, but the shipyard had made up the time it had lost at the start of the project. The ship's condensers were installed, and work to attach the upper deck had begun. With ninety percent of the pre-launch construction work completed, the structure on the slipway was beginning to look like a battleship.

On May 4 Watanabe received notification from the Bureau of Naval Construction that the Yokosuka Arsenal had held a small ceremony that day to mark the start of construction on the No. 3 Battleship.

# 14

# In the Belly of the Beast

**Summer 1940**

On July 3, 1940, Ogawa and Watanabe accompanied Lieutenant Commander Kajiwara on a visit to the Bureau of Naval Construction in Tokyo. Installation work on the launch platform had already begun, and the launch date was now only four months away. The object of the visit was to discuss how the shipyard would maintain the secrecy of the project during and after the launch.

The hemp screens had hidden the battleship during its construction, but when launched, the vessel would emerge from the hemp cage into the middle of the harbor. During the subsequent phase, when the vessel would be in the Mukaijima dock for the year or so it would take to complete the outfitting, the huge warship would be as visible as the harbor itself. It seemed that all the care that the shipyard had taken to hide the battleship while it was on the slipway would be rendered completely meaningless after the launch.

The meeting at headquarters was chaired by Vice Admiral Soemu Toyoda. An officer from the General Affairs Division handed each of the participants an agenda for the day's meeting.

They moved to the first item: Preserving secrecy during the launch.

Once the No. 2 Battleship is in the Mukaijima outfitting dock, it can be shielded by hemp blinds, but during the launch, the battleship's hull will be in full view, with no immediate means of hiding it. If the hull of the No. 2 Battleship were to be photographed, the enemy would not only be informed of the specifics of the No. 2 Battleship, but also of the No. 1 and No. 3 battleships. Therefore, it is vital that we come up with some measure to hide the hull of the No. 2 Battleship at this critical time.

The launch of a ship was usually accompanied by a ceremony, but the shipyard had taken special precautions with the No. 2 Battleship. The day of the launch was to be kept secret from everyone but top shipyard and Navy officials. The launch would follow tradition, but quietly.

"We understand why you are worried," Toyoda began. "Those attending the ceremony from the Navy will be limited to the chief of the Naval General Staff, His Highness Prince Fushimi, the minister of the Navy, the director of the Sasebo Naval Station, and myself.

"We have asked all the participants to come to Nagasaki in civilian clothes, so as not to attract the attention of the local population. The launch ceremony itself will also be greatly abridged: There will be no performance of the National Anthem or the Battleship March, and streamers and confetti will not be used."

The meeting shifted to the second item on the agenda: Visually shielding the battleship after launch.

Ogawa opened the discussion. "We are researching various means of hiding the ship during the launch, but we have as yet nothing to report."

"What about the smokescreen idea we discussed earlier?" Toyoda asked.

About six months earlier the Navy had suggested that the shipyard use a smokescreen to hide the battleship during the launch. After exhaustive testing, however, the shipyard had abandoned the idea because it was too dependent on weather conditions. Ogawa explained the drawbacks of a smokescreen, and Toyoda nodded.

"The launch at Kure is no problem," Toyoda said, "but the launch area and outfitting dock in Nagasaki are right in the middle of the city."

The general affairs director scowled, and the room fell into an uncomfortable silence.

"This is where I have a favor to ask," Kajiwara finally said. "I have already discussed this matter with President Ogawa and Project Director Watanabe. Whatever means we try to hide the ship will not be as effective as the hemp blinds shielding it while it is on the slipway. Therefore, we have decided that the only way to preserve the secrecy of the project is to make sure that no undesirable person is within view of the vessel during the launch."

Kajiwara took a deep breath and continued, "We have already established several observation posts in the heights around Nagasaki. The citizens are now so afraid of being arrested that they deliberately avoid even looking in the direction of the shipyard. But even this is not enough. Our patrol forces are understaffed. If a foreign spy were in Nagasaki during the launch, he might easily photograph the battleship without being caught. This problem is a matter of the gravest importance, and we would request that the Navy dispatch a task force to patrol the city during and after the launch."

Toyoda remained silent for a moment and stared out the window, considering the request. Finally he said, "Of course, this is not just a Navy problem, but one which affects the entire nation. How many men do you need?"

"One thousand at the very least," Kajiwara answered quickly.

"Very well," said Toyoda. "I'll draft a ministerial order right away."

Kajiwara looked relieved and smiled at his civilian colleagues. The meeting moved on to the next item: Hiding the battleship from the United States and British consulates.

Ogawa used a blackboard to describe the relationship of the two consulates to the No. 2 slipway and the outfitting dock. The No. 2 slipway was slightly to the left of the consulates, but the Mukaijima outfitting dock was directly opposite and only 650 meters away.

"We have put a great deal of thought into methods of concealing the battleship from the consulates," Ogawa said, "and have come to the conclusion that the only effective measure would be to build a structure in front of the consulates to block their view."

The first idea had been to build a fourteen-meter-high billboard on the beach. But after further consideration, the shipyard realized that such a billboard might be blown over by strong winds, not to mention the fact that a huge billboard with no apparent practical purpose might invite suspicion.

The final solution to the problem had come from an unlikely quarter: a proposal from the Nagasaki Public Works Department to build a storehouse on the beach. After discussing the procurement of the lumber needed to build the storehouse, the meeting moved on to more specific details of the launch and outfitting.

The meeting decided that all traffic in Nagasaki harbor would be banned on the day of the launch, and that the controlled areas around the city would be expanded. Finally, two Navy counter-intelligence specialists would be sent to the city to determine how to ensure the secrecy of the project during and after the crucial day.

*     *     *

After returning to Nagasaki on the night train, Kajiwara gave a detailed report of the proceedings to Shimamoto, who began looking for ways to expand the areas under supervision on the heights around Nagasaki.

Using the binoculars in the observation posts at the No. 2 slipway, the Mukaijima outfitting dock, and on the roof of the naval supervisors' office, Kajiwara drew a line around a map of Nagasaki, designating areas that might have a view of the launch and outfitting areas. He then contacted the military and local police, asking them to put up billboards announcing the new restricted areas.

Just as these preparations were finished, Shimamoto received a coded telegram from the Bureau of Naval Construction informing him that a 1,200-man patrol force would be sent from the Sasebo

Naval Station in mid-October. A separate message added that two counter-intelligence specialists would arrive in the near future.

At the beginning of July a man working on the No. 2 Battleship lost his footing and fell to the concrete slipway below. He went into a coma and died three hours later. The incident was a bad omen to shipyard executives, and they were not surprised when a typhoon arrived several days later to ravage the entire island of Kyushu. Navy and shipyard officials feared that the storm might cause irreparable damage to the slipway and the hull, and to their dismay the typhoon was the strongest Nagasaki had seen in years.

After an emergency meeting Watanabe and his men walked through the rain to the slipway, where they filed into the massive dark hull of the battleship. Their worst fear was that the screens would be torn down by the hurricane-force winds of the typhoon.

The interior of the battleship's hull was silent despite the storm raging outside. Periodically, the men would venture up to a deck immediately below the main deck and listen to the howling winds and torrential rains pounding against the deck plates and vibrating them like a massive steel drum. The group kept an all-night vigil in the ship on one of the lower decks.

When dawn finally broke, the winds seemed to have abated a little. Watanabe and some of the others put on hard hats and raincoats and ventured topside. The spectacle on deck was strange and violent. Hemp screens were waving in huge sweeps of wind, and the noise from the gantry cranes was like the mad rustling of the leaves in a grove of giant trees.

Most of the aluminum plates that had been attached to the bottom of the cranes had been ripped off by the wind. On the main deck, immediately in front of the men peering from the hatch, the aluminum plates seemed to be dancing in the wind.

Watanabe divided his men into groups and sent them around the deck to check for damage. As he looked around, he felt a bit more at ease. As far as he could see from his vantage point, the screens were all still firmly attached to the gantry cranes. When the men returned, they reported that the blinds had been blown away in two places on the harbor side and in one place near the ship's port bow.

"I guess hemp blinds were the right choice after all," Watanabe said with a weary sigh of relief.

# 15
## Day of the Dead

**Summer 1940**

The sun shone brightly over Nagasaki on July 14 and 15, the days of the summer *Bon* Festival. On the fourteenth the citizens of Nagasaki would climb the slopes around the city to visit their family graves and place lanterns in front of the grave stones. By nightfall a glorious curtain of light would cover the hills, which would reflect off the streams of incense drifting over the graves and into the sky. On the night of the fifteenth the *joryobune* boats carrying the souls of the dead would float down the rivers and out to bay.

That same night workers began rearranging the hemp screens on the harbor side of the No. 2 slipway. The screens were attached vertically, and the resulting single huge blind was fastened to a thick overhead rope. The work took all night, and as morning approached workers realized that the pulleys and ropes they had installed would be used to roll the screen like an enormous window blind just before the battleship slid, stern first, into the harbor.

The workers, however, were skeptical that the heavy hemp blind could be raised in time for the launch. On the other hand, if the blind were raised too early, the battleship would be visible from the outside. An additional visual barrier, consisting of two large canvas sheets, was hung over the slipway portal. The sheets were designed to open like theater curtains once the blind was raised. When everything was in place, the mechanisms for raising the blind and opening the curtains were tested nightly to ensure they functioned properly. The time it took to raise the blinds and open the curtains was carefully recorded during each trial.

On August 8 news reached the shipyard that the No. 1 Battleship had been launched without complications from its dock in Kure. Construction, which had started on November 4, 1937, had taken two years and nine months. Despite the relatively easy conditions of the No. 1 Battleship's launch, the Navy engineers had spent a considerable amount of time making sure the unusual size and weight of the hull would not create any complications. Their calculations proved accurate, and the huge hull lifted off the floor of the dock and was towed out into the harbor.

* * *

In early September the hull of the No. 2 Battleship was painted gray, and in October the chrysanthemum insignia was lifted into place at the bow. From then on workers on the No. 2 slipway concentrated on pre-launch preparations.

The hull was now over twenty meters high, and its six-deck interior was already equipped with all of its major machinery. The only thing left was to slide the giant 36,000-ton structure off the slipway into the sea.

The hull was held stable by a multitude of wooden blocks around the keel and thick support beams propping up the sides. The four-meter launch rails, which had been inserted between the blocks under the hull, looked like two wide sled blades running the entire length of the ship.

Just before the launch, the blocks and support beams would be gradually removed, and the weight of the battleship shifted onto the launch platform. The two launch rails would then slide the ship into the harbor.

On October 15 workers began removing parts from the battleship in order to lighten it for the launch. These included the front and rear bridges, which had been attached for reference, and the deck plates that had been laid under the ship's smokestack. This reduced the weight to 35,737 tons.

By that time a total of 5.4 million rivets and twenty-six kilometers of welded seams held the hull together. The final launch weight had been calculated to the last rivet.

The narrowness of the harbor at the launch site was what worried the engineers most. According to Hamada's calculations, the 263-meter-long battleship would slide stern-first at fifteen knots (approximately twenty-eight kilometers per hour). And unless the 36,000-ton hull could be slowed, it would crash into the opposite shore one and a half minutes later, destroying all of the buildings on the far bank and grounding itself like a huge beached whale.

At first Watanabe had thought the battleship could be made to veer to the left by attaching chains to the port side, but after various calculations and experiments, Hamada realized that the dynamics of the launch were not nearly so simple. The weight of the battleship was much too great for even the heaviest chains to alter its trajectory.

A series of pre-launch meetings held in Watanabe's office concentrated on how to prevent the No. 2 Battleship from running aground. How could they, in just a minute and a half, alter the course of 36,000 tons of steel?

The solution the engineers finally came up with was to attach an equal number of chains to both sides of the ship. They calculated that with 285 tons of chains attached to the starboard and port sides, to create a total anchoring weight of 570 tons, the hull should come to a halt about 220 meters from the opposite shore. As a further precaution, the hull would be tethered to a line of buoys by a thick steel cable.

On paper the sums worked out perfectly, but on the day many things could go wrong: The chains could break, or the cable connecting the ship to the buoys could snap. In order to minimize the damage to the hull if it did run aground, a large wooden raft was moored to the opposite shore to act as buffer.

The shipyard borrowed twelve chains from naval arsenals around Japan to get the desired weight of 570 tons. The procedure of fastening the chains to the battleship began on October 16. The twelve chains were strung away from the ship's sides toward the harbor, in the direction the ship would slide during the launch.

At the same time two twenty-five-meter steel rods were installed on the sides of the vessel, slightly fore of midships. The rods, which had been designed to move freely up and down and from left to right, were hung with hemp blinds. Their function was to hide the scale of the battleship once it was in the harbor.

Watanabe and his team then discussed means of keeping the entire launch secret. Their first problem was how to hide the all-night work session on the eve of the launch. Preparations for the launch of any ship started at dusk and continued until the next morning. The preparations for the No. 2 Battleship launch would be no different, but lights burning throughout the night might alert any interested parties.

Watanabe decided to start all-night work sessions some time before the actual day of the launch, making such work the norm instead of the exception and confusing any outside observers as to the actual date of the event. The all-night sessions began two weeks before November 1, and lights shone brightly inside the hemp cage every night until dawn.

The slipway workers sensed that the launch was imminent from the tension on the faces of their superiors. The pre-launch inspections of the hull were carried out on October 22 and 23, further strengthening the workers' suspicions. But there was still no official announcement about the exact date and time of the launch.

# 16

# Glimpse of the Abyss

**Autumn 1940**

Dusk had descended on the shipyard. Wrapped in darkness, the huge vessel seemed to stretch out endlessly. Watanabe looked up at the hull looming above him. The curved mass of steel looked like it had been sitting there for hundreds of years. He wondered if it would really move on November 1, as the launch calculations predicted it would.

"It's only when I walk along the slipway that I realize how enormous this ship is," Koga said in wonder. Watanabe and Kajiwara only nodded silently.

The next day, after the final inspection of the battleship, the entire vessel was cleaned in preparation for the launch. The workers entered the ship's hull in the morning with their lunch boxes and did not emerge until late that evening.

The vast interior of the battleship was a complicated maze of tunnels and compartments. On several occasions shipyard workers got lost inside. Carrying white chalk with them so they could mark the way out, the working parties took a roll call upon entering and exiting the vessel to be sure that no one had been left behind.

On October 26, as the morning bell rang signalling the start of the work day, Watanabe called the heads of all the shipyard divisions involved in the project to an emergency meeting at the No. 2 slipway. He announced that until the launch was over, no one without a special armband would be permitted to enter the slipway for any reason.

He then handed out armbands embossed with a cherry blossom

insignia to the division heads who were directly involved in the launch and sent all of the others back to their posts. About 1,000 slipway workers were issued with armbands, along with additional surveying personnel and others due to be let in on the day of the launch.

No one explained the new security crackdown to the workers, who were growing increasingly nervous with the odd developments of the pre-launch period. Frightened, they obediently followed orders given by the supervisors still allowed on the slipway. They hurriedly went about their duties, making last minute inspections of the launch platform.

On October 30 workers went through a full launch rehearsal. All preparations had been completed, and a ceremonial platform had been built directly in front of the glistening ship's bow. Watanabe felt suddenly dizzy when he looked down over the slipway from the observation deck. He had not been able to sleep properly for weeks. If he chanced to drift off, nightmarish visions of the battleship turning over wrenched him awake again. The whiteness of the slipway prepared for the launch was eerily reminiscent of the scene in his nightmares.

There was no second chance with a launch. The slightest mistake could create a catastrophic and irreversible accident. In his obsession with failure, Watanabe had researched the history of such catastrophes at the shipyard.

On June 5, 1915, the Nagasaki Shipyard held the launch ceremony for the 9,506-ton *Manila-maru*, a commercial vessel commissioned by the Osaka Steamship Company. The ceremonies were conducted according to procedure, and the restraining nets were cut. The ship's hull stood fast on the slipway. Flanked by a representative of the company that had commissioned the vessel, Taisuke Shioda, shipyard president at the time, was embarrassed by the unexpected complication.

The stunned Shioda turned to the assembled dignitaries and said, "Let us drink a toast in the hope that the *Manila-maru* will soon slide obediently into the sea."

The launch ceremony was thus carried out with the hull still sitting on the slipway. The ship was finally coaxed into the sea the next day, but Watanabe worried that this had only been possible because the *Manila-maru* was a relatively small ship. If such a slipup occurred with the No. 2 Battleship, the problem might not be solved so easily. He was afraid that one failure would make any further attempts at launching the ship impossible. The vast battleship would simply sit on the No. 2 slipway for eternity.

On April 27, 1937, another unsuccessful launch had taken place at the shipyard, this time taking the life of one worker and injuring many others. The 7,363-ton *Ooryoku-maru* was, again, a vessel commissioned by the Osaka Steamship Company. Just before the ceremony was due to begin, and workers were making the final preparations, the massive hull began to slide off the slipway without warning.

A worker who was on deck as the hull began to move was caught up in one of the restraining ropes. His legs were cut off at the thighs, and he was thrown far out into the sea in the direction the ship was sliding. Other workers managed to rescue the injured man, but he died later of blood loss.

Watanabe wondered what the consequences would be on the slipway if the battleship began to slide before the prescribed time. The slipway portal would still be covered by the hemp blind, and the curtains in front of that would also be closed. The battleship would rip through the hemp blind and the curtains. Anyone on deck or near the hull at the time would be swept away, and many valuable lives would be lost, including the team of engineers who would still be on the deck making preparations.

An even worse scenario was for the battleship to hit the hemp blinds and pull down the gantry cranes to which they were attached. Workers would be crushed, and the ship's hull would be severely damaged.

Tables covered in snow-white tablecloths were already lined up on the platform at the ship's bow, and Watanabe realized that not just the expectations of the Navy, but those of the entire nation rested on a successful launch. For a moment, as he gazed down from the observation deck above the slipway, Watanabe felt he could hardly breathe.

* * *

That night a ship coasted silently into Nagasaki Bay and docked at one of the harbor buoys. Several hours later 1,200 Navy troops spilled out onto the ship's deck, jumped into lifeboats, and rowed ashore. These troops were the special patrol officers Kajiwara had requested from the Navy. They had been trained at the Sasebo Naval Station on the specifics of patrolling Nagasaki during the launch.

A light rain was falling, and the shipyard docks were dark. After a quick roll call the patrolmen split off into several groups and disappeared into the darkness.

As dawn broke on the morning of October 31, 1940, a deep late-autumn red filled the sky. The entrances to the No. 2 slipway were sealed at 9 A.M. Watanabe forbade all employees without armbands to enter the area and announced that no one would be permitted to return home that night. Most of the workers had not even been told about the details of the launch, and they were overwhelmed by the thought of trying to move the monstrous hull. They nervously finished the final cleaning, uncertain of what they were expected to do next.

A special meeting of all workers on the slipway was called shortly after lunch on October 31. Over 600 engineers and workers gathered for what was, for most, the first instructions they had received about the launch.

At exactly 2:00 P.M. Watanabe stepped up onto a small podium and addressed the assembled workers.

"This battleship will be launched tomorrow morning at 8:55," he announced. "The launch director will be Masanao Serikawa "

Watanabe's round face was flushed with excitement. A silence enveloped the crowd of workers. The entire launch crew stared at him, but no one reacted—waiting for more.

Watanabe stepped down, making way for Serikawa, who pulled a sheaf of notes from his breast pocket.

"As launch director," he began, "I would like to raise one or two points. In contrast to the previous launches you have taken part in, this launch is of primary importance to the security of the nation. Its success or failure will not only have a direct effect on the reputation of this shipyard, but it will also reflect the shipbuilding technology of the Japanese Empire.

"Of course, the many years of experience of our workers, the painstaking years of research of our engineers, and the superior technological capabilities of this shipyard give us the utmost confidence that we shall succeed. We should all, however, endeavor to do our best in whatever function we perform during this operation. Those who have the privilege of working on this project today will be able to talk about it with pride to their children and grandchildren. This project is the very embodiment of a man's pride in his work.

"Preparations for the launch will begin today at 4:30. It will involve more than 1,000 people. Concentrate on your own work and listen to the directions of your supervisors. Perform your allotted tasks calmly and carefully. I want all 1,000 of you to become one unified team to get this job done. Success depends upon it. In conclusion, let us all bow to the east to pray for a successful launch."

With Serikawa's final words, all of the workers turned to the east and bowed.

Serikawa then called a meeting of the heads of each shipyard division and explained the procedures of the launch operation.

Finally, the command was given.

"Begin launch preparations," Serikawa shouted shrilly.

Workers dispersed and began the work of installing the safety devices designed to prevent the battleship from sliding off the slipway before the prescribed time.

The launch structure consisted of a sliding platform and a stationary platform. The stationary platform was made up of two rails fastened securely to the concrete slipway. On top of these rested the launch runners—the sliding platform that moved with the ship. The shipyard had already put eighteen tons of resin, seven tons of vegetable fat, and two tons of soft soap between the platforms. Many of the workers were certain that, with all the lubricants used, the battleship would begin sliding as soon as the hull was shifted off the support blocks—no matter what kind of safety measures were taken.

At 4:30 P.M. workers began to remove the wooden blocks holding the battleship on the slipway, along with the beams supporting the ship's sides. The weight of the battleship was slowly shifted onto the rails. First the keel blocks were pulled from the very bottom of the ship, then the workers moved slowly up each side.

As the sun set the slipway was lit by blinding electric lights attached to the top of the gantry cranes. Hundreds of workers, foreheads wrapped in headbands, and bodies sweating profusely, continued removing the countless support blocks. The removal work was a race against time. High tide was at 8:55 the following morning and, if for some reason they were unable to make this deadline, the next high tide would not come for almost two more days. It would be impossible to stabilize the ship on the launch rails for that long. Once the process of removing the blocks had begun, there was no turning back.

The night air turned cold. Watanabe, Kajiwara, and Koga stood below the bow of the ship, supervising the work. They were thankful that the removal of the supports was proceeding according to schedule. The workers as yet showed no signs of tiring.

The workers' evening meal was lowered into the slipway by one of the gantry cranes. They greedily ate their rations during the fifteen-minute meal break and immediately returned to work.

As the moon rose high in the late-October sky, the pace of work quickened.

The first crisis hit at about 1:00 A.M. A messenger from the far side of the slipway ran frantically toward Watanabe. His face was white with panic. Watanabe braced himself for bad news.

"The floor of the slipway is splitting!" the man blurted out.

The three men were soon running behind the messenger to the scene.

Serikawa, Hamada, and Omiya were already surveying the huge cracks in the concrete. Watanabe looked at the slipway floor where Hamada was pointing. He gasped. Two deep fractures had formed between the launch rails.

The layer of concrete covering the slipway was a meter thick, with steel plates bolted into it. But as the support blocks were gradually removed, the battleship's weight had been concentrated on the rails, causing the area between them to give way.

The weight of the battleship once again astounded Watanabe. He remembered the catastrophic launch scene he had seen so many times in his nightmares. The cold night air gusted by the director, making him shudder. If the slipway floor continued to split, the ship's hull would capsize, smashing the huge gantry cranes on one side. With the force of the fall, the 27,700-ton *Kashihara-maru* on the neighboring slipway would also be destroyed, and the entire shipyard would be paralyzed.

Watanabe's knees were shaking uncontrollably. He watched Omiya's face closely as he inspected the fissures in the bed of the slipway, hoping to discover how serious the problem really was. Omiya pointed his flashlight into the cracks as he walked along; Watanabe and the others followed silently behind him.

Omiya finally looked up and said in a slightly shaken voice, "It looks like it's going to hold. I don't think it will crack any further."

Watanabe bent over to peer into the cracks, "Are you sure?" he asked.

Omiya looked calmer, and his expression returned to normal.

105

"It's probably all right. The split runs along the seam connecting the old slipway to the expanded portion. It has given as much as it is going to, I think. We don't have to worry about it getting any larger."

Watanabe sighed.

# 17

# A Delicate Balance

**Autumn 1940**

"Koga," Watanabe said, regaining his composure. "Stay here and keep an eye on the cracks. Don't let the workers know that the slipway floor has split."

The remaining wooden supports were quickly removed from the bottom of the ship. Watanabe noticed an uncomfortable dryness in his mouth as he supervised the operation. Gradually, more and more of the battleship's weight was being shifted to the launching rails. He expected the slipway to give out at any moment and a piercing sound to fill the air as the cracks ran longer and deeper.

Every five minutes messengers would run between Watanabe and Koga to report on the condition of the cracks. But just as Omiya had predicted, they showed no signs of getting any larger.

At 3:00 A.M. the hemp blind was rolled up, right on schedule. As the huge blind slowly lifted, the thick canvas sheets of the outer curtain appeared behind it.

The eastern sky began to whiten. Over ten hours had passed since preparations had begun. A look of deep fatigue had begun to set on the faces of the half-naked workers, whose bodies were blackened with dirt, sweat, and oil. Bloodshot eyes shone eerily from hundreds of black faces.

The tide was slowly rising, and the water beneath the ship's bow began to reflect the red of the rising sun.

Serikawa was running busily around the ship's bow. "It's almost time," he shouted, his voice hoarse from the strain.

The workers seemed to be so exhausted that Watanabe expected them to collapse, but they somehow managed to tap hidden energy reserves and continue.

As dawn approached the visiting Navy dignitaries gathered to attend the launch. Several thousand guests would normally attend the launch of a battleship, but, as promised, only about thirty had been sent to attend the ceremony.

The chief of the Naval General Staff, Prince Fushimi, had arrived the night before in civilian clothes and stayed with several attendants in a special guest house inside the shipyard. The guests from the Bureau of Naval Construction, Vice Admiral Toyoda and Vice Admiral Kuwabara, had brought an entourage of several officers each. They spent the night at an inn two stops from Nagasaki's central station.

The two groups had taken great pains before leaving Tokyo to break up into several smaller parties and to travel on separate trains. The senior officers made frequent trips from Tokyo to Nagasaki and were well known to the stewards on the express trains. In order to avoid being recognized, they took different routes to Nagasaki: Some changed trains at Kure, while others traveled to Sasebo and finished the journey by ship.

The group from the Sasebo Naval Station, including the station's commanding officer, Vice Admiral Noboru Hirata, arrived in Nagasaki the same night and stayed in an inn just outside the city so as not to attract attention. Later that night they took a car to the shipyard.

Navy Minister Koshiro Oikawa and his staff arrived in Nagasaki at 7:29 A.M. The unmarked car that took the minister's party from the station to the shipyard picked the least crowded streets and whisked the minister, unnoticed, to the scene of the launch. Only two local officials were permitted to attend: the governor of Nagasaki Prefecture and the chief of the prefectural police.

By dawn 1,800 men were on patrol in the streets of Nagasaki. The two Navy counter-intelligence specialists, who had been in Nagasaki for over a month, had been researching effective ways of hiding the launch from the city's residents. They knew it would be impossible to keep the launch secret if people were allowed to wander freely in the streets. On the other hand, the residents would be suspicious if they were forced to stay indoors without a valid reason. Most would probably suspect the commotion had something to do with whatever ship was behind the hemp screens in the shipyard. The Navy decided it had to think of a way to keep people in their homes that day, and the specialists had recommended an air-raid drill as the best way.

Patrol officers could be seen everywhere in the hills and city streets, but even they had been ordered to turn their backs to the harbor when the ship was launched, so they would not see the shape and size of the vessel.

The officers were instructed to be especially thorough with the communities along the coast. Each family was ordered to stay indoors; the rain shutters of the Japanese-style houses were to be shut, and the curtains drawn on Western-style windows. Several patrol officers were assigned to each house to keep careful watch on the residents' activities.

The Navy had spent a great deal of time researching ways of hiding the launch from Nagasaki's foreign residents. Except for the Chinese, the police were restricted by diplomatic agreements from forcing foreign residents to cooperate with them. Counter-intelligence was naturally much more concerned about foreigners witnessing the launch than about Japanese seeing it. After a great deal of research, it came up with two methods of dealing with the problem.

The *Kasuga-maru*, a 17,127-ton freighter commissioned by the Nippon Yusen Company, had recently been launched at the shipyard and was being outfitted at one of the quays. The freighter would be towed in front of the No. 2 slipway immediately after the launch. The freighter was much smaller than the battleship, but if it could be used to hide even a portion of the hull, it would prevent observers from getting a good idea of the shape and scale of the entire vessel.

In order to ensure that foreign residents would not be able to watch the launch, two officers would visit each foreign household immediately before the event, saying they had been ordered to make a house inspection. The officers had orders to drag the inspection out and divert the foreigners' attention away from the harbor.

The morning of November 1 finally broke. The city lay in silence, and a mist covered the harbor. Small columns of smoke from kitchen fires rose from many homes. The special patrol officers were already at their posts, with men lining the shore at ten meter intervals. The policemen assigned to the homes of foreigners were waiting for 8:30 A.M. to begin their house calls. In the harbor, the *Kasuga-maru* was ready to shield the battleship after it slid into the water.

The tide was slowly rising. Launch preparations were still approaching their final, furious stages inside the slipway. The process of shifting the enormous weight of the hull onto the launch rails was almost finished. The voices of the supervisors at each observation point were hoarse from shouting. Everyone's eyes were bloodshot from lack of sleep.

At 8:10 A.M. Serikawa stood to attention in front of Watanabe and announced the completion of launch preparations. About ten of the wooden blocks under the ship's keel had been left to stabilize the hull.

Engineers swarmed over the ship's deck in order to survey the launch. They had already been warned that the ship would be launched on schedule, even if the curtains over the slipway portal could not be opened in time. The pointed stern would rip through the thick canvas, and the vessel would slide out into the ocean regardless of the obstacle. But the curtain would flap violently over the battleship, and anyone on deck at the time would be swept overboard. The men had been ordered to prepare a shelter in case this happened.

When the hull slid along the slipway it would pull with it the twelve anchoring chains. Watanabe now worried that the chains might somehow get tangled up in the huge steel columns of the gantry cranes on either side of the slipway and pull them down.

After announcing the end of launch preparations, Serikawa ordered all section supervisors on the slipway to assume launch positions.

At 8:20 A.M. the guests from the Bureau of Naval Construction and Sasebo Naval Station were led into the slipway by Shimamoto. Prince Fushimi and Navy Minister Koshiro Oikawa arrived and changed into their uniforms. They climbed onto the platform in front of the ship's bow.

The huge hull stood waiting to slide off the launch rails in the silent absence of a military band and surrounded by 1,000 shipyard workers who, after a full night's work, stood motionless and exhausted, looking up at the distant figures of the Navy officers on the platform above them.

At 8:30 A.M. Ogawa told Navy Minister Oikawa that all prelaunch preparations had been completed. Oikawa opened an envelope and began to read the official naming declaration for the battleship in a cold, ceremonial tone.

"This battleship..., construction of which commenced on March 29, 1938, is ready to be launched."

Ogawa was unnerved by the speech. Oikawa had said "this battleship," but he could not make out the name that followed. The minister had definitely said something, but so quickly and quietly that no one could hear it clearly. Ogawa realized that this was the Navy's way of keeping the battleship's name secret, even from the workers who were attending the ceremony.

Serikawa bowed to the guests of honor, then looked down at the 1,000 workers on the dock. He raised his hands, and shouted, "Begin the launch!"

The silence was immediately broken. The 1,000 workers who had stood stock still throughout the ceremony broke into unified activity. They began to remove the wooden blocks that remained around the keel. It was almost high tide, and seawater was now splashing against the stern. The precise time for the launch was drawing near.

Finally, the engineer in charge of signalling the start of the launch raised his white pennant and swept it down with a powerful stroke.

Nagasaki Harbor *(Mitsubishi Heavy Industries)*

Nagasaki Shipyard *(Mitsubishi Heavy Industries)*

Kensuke Watanabe
*(Mitsubishi Heavy Industries)*

The sinking of the *Tosa* after Japan signed the Washington Treaty *(Koji Ito)*

The storehouse built to hide the launch of the *Musashi* from the British and American consulates *(Mitsubishi Heavy Industries)*

The outfitting of the *Yamato* at the Kure Arsenal *(Shizuo Fukui)*

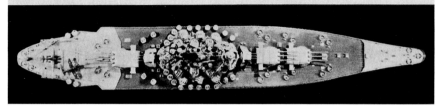

↑ 23. 対空兵装改装後の武蔵模型船外側面写真。 (三菱造船提供)
↑ 23. Side view of a miniature model of BB *Musashi* after the reinforcement of anti-aircraft armaments.

↓ 24. 対空兵装改装後の武蔵模型上部平面写真。 (三菱造船提供)
↓ 24. Vertical view of a miniature model of BB *Musashi* after the reinforcement of anti-aircraft armaments.

A scale model of the *Musashi* after the reinforcement of its anti-aircraft armament *(Mitsubishi Heavy Industries)*

The No. 1 and No. 2 main gun turrets and the No. 1 auxiliary gun turret *(Shizuo Fukui)*

12.7 cm anti-aircraft guns *(Shizuo Fukui)*

12.7 cm anti-aircraft guns
*(Shizuo Fukui)*

The No. 1 bridge and one of the 46-cm guns
*(Shizuo Fukui)*

The No. 1 bridge and conning tower
*(Shiryo Chosakai)*

The hangar, launching catapults, and crane for *Musashi*'s six planes *(Shizuo Fukui)*

The *Yamato* and the *Musashi* at the Truk Island anchorage *(Shizuo Fukui)*

Admiral Isoroku Yamamoto

The fleet at anchor in Brunei Bay in October 1944 *(KK Bestsellers)*

The *Musashi* making its final sortie from Brunei Bay on October 22, 1944
*(Shizuo Fukui)*

The *Musashi* listing heavily to port. It sank in the Sibuyan Sea at 7:15P.M.,
on October 24, 1944 *(Shuppan Kyodo Publishers)*

# 18
# The Launch

November 1, 1940

Serikawa struck the launching bell. Two groups of workers rushed to either side of the keel to remove the last remaining blocks.

"Blocks have been removed from under the keel," Serikawa yelled to Ogawa.

Flagposts had been attached to several turrets equally spaced along the length of the ship. One by one, white flags unfurled on the starboard side.

Serikawa rang the second bell. "Blocks on the starboard side have been removed," he shouted.

Next, the flags unfurled on the port side. The third bell rang.

"The port side supports have been removed," Serikawa yelled, his voice cracking under the strain. "Open the curtains!"

Watanabe held his breath. As the curtains began to part, the hills on the far shore of the harbor appeared in the mist. His heart was beating frantically. Once the curtains were fully opened, the harbor came into view—the first time the sea had been seen from the slipway in over two and a half years.

After confirming that the curtains had been completely opened, Serikawa yelled for the workers to release the safeties on the launch rails. Men surrounded the launch platform and removed the remaining safety devices locking the sliding and stationary rails. The piercing sound of the fourth bell reverberated over the slipway.

"Safety devices have been removed," Serikawa yelled to Ogawa.

Ogawa lifted a silver axe to cut the rope holding the giant hull to the No. 2 slipway. Two years and eight months of construction work and nineteen hours of launch preparations had finally ended. The ship only waited for Ogawa to lower his axe on the last remaining tether.

A deep silence enveloped the slipway. Watanabe opened his eyes wide for this final moment, wondering if one slash of an axe was really going to move the huge vessel.

Ogawa stood in the shadow of the battleship's hull. He bowed to Prince Fushimi. The axe glinted in his hands as he raised it, and he brought it down powerfully onto the rope.

Watanabe looked back at the vast hull of the battleship. He held his breath, staring intently. The ship was not moving! His mind clouded over in panic until he noticed a slight movement. He stared closely at one section of the hull where he had detected motion and prayed that he would see more. After a few seconds he realized that the movement was not a hallucination. The ship was really moving.

A strange heat welled up inside Watanabe.

Soundlessly the battleship started its slide over the launch platform. As it picked up speed, the chains attached to the sides began to bounce over the concrete, their rattle growing louder, until it became a deafening roar. A startling shower of sparks erupted between the chains and the slipway.

The heat from Watanabe's chest rose into his throat, and he was momentarily unable to breathe.

The whole slipway shook violently and filled with dust and smoke. Several workers shouted *Banzai!* After the first cries, other workers raised their hands and cheered. To Watanabe, who had been having bad dreams about a catastrophe for the past two years, the cheers sounded like the screams of the dying men in his nightmares.

The heat rising from Watanabe's chest reached his face. As the stern hit the water, it sent up a dramatic spray of foam. The sound of the water and the roar of the chains drowned out the cries of the workers.

The resins that had been spread on top of the stationary runners began to heat up under the tremendous weight of the battleship, and the rails gave off white smoke.

The battleship had moved completely free of the slipway and was careening at considerable speed across the harbor with the surveying team standing on the main deck. Huge waves engulfed both sides of the hull, and the twelve chains attached to the ship's sides tumbled heavily into the water.

Watanabe was suddenly struck by a new fear that the battleship was going to run aground. The hull already blocked his view of the hills, and Watanabe imagined it continuing on its course and ramming into the opposite shore.

But the ship gradually slowed, and it finally came to a halt, its stern pointing slightly to the west. The cheers of the workers on the slipway began to settle, and a wave of joyful sobbing swept over the launch area. Eyes shining, the workers watched the guests descend from the platform. After the last guest had departed, their cheers became louder and stronger. It was as though the accumulated exhaustion of the previous night and the hundreds of days preceding it had been released in one giant surge of emotion. Engineers collapsed on deck, pulling one another down as they embraced.

The three launch engineers—Serikawa, Hamada, and Omiya —ran to Watanabe. Unable to speak, they simply bowed and wept. Watanabe and the others turned toward the harbor. Though they had spent the past two and a half years working on the project, it was the first time they had seen the complete hull of the battleship. It was startlingly large—many times larger than anything they had imagined from the blueprints.

The water level in the harbor after the launch was over fifty centimeters higher than at high tide, an unforeseen effect of the huge volume and weight of the battleship. The launch raised a 120-centimeter wave, which crashed against the coast in the Naminohira district along the bay with the force of a tidal wave. Residents in the area were locked inside their homes because of the air-raid drill when a wave of seawater washed up under the foundations of their homes and through the tatami floor mats. Those who fled their homes in panic were ordered back inside by police officers and were forced to remain in their flooded houses until later that evening.

The huge wave also surged up the Urakami, Oura, and Nakashima rivers, flooding homes along the banks and capsizing small fishing boats.

The *Kasuga-maru* drifted slowly alongside the No. 2 Battleship. When it reached the larger vessel, the long perpendicular rods that had been installed on the battleship's sides were deployed as planned. The rods stuck out like wings, screening the battleship from the city.

Seven tugboats gathered in front of the No. 2 Battleship. In perfect synchronization with the *Kasuga-maru*, they pulled the hull across the harbor to the Mukaijima outfitting dock. By midday the battleship was docked and awaiting the final stage of construction.

# 19
# Fire!

**Autumn 1940**


On the following evening a few of the shipyard's top executives gathered at a city-center restaurant to celebrate the successful launch. Now that the hull was afloat, the bulk of the construction work had been finished.

The launch had been perfect. The battleship had come to a halt 221 meters from the opposite shore of the harbor, only one meter off from the calculations made by the launch engineers. They were also blessed with good weather. If it had been raining, the soft soap used to lubricate the launch rails might have been washed away; if it had been too windy, the surface of the harbor would have become choppy, which could have greatly impeded the launch. Even the fact that there was a mist on the harbor that morning helped preserve the secrecy of the launch. Watanabe personally thanked Hamada and Omiya, whose years of painstaking research had handsomely paid off.

After the national holiday celebrating Emperor Meiji's birthday on November 3, workers began the final stage of construction: the outfitting of the ship. The hull, which had been given its flesh and bones, would now be fitted with its internal organs and circulatory system.

Before the outfitting began, Watanabe summoned the project engineers to his office to tell them that the Navy had asked him to bring forward the battleship's completion date from December to July 1942. With the worsening international situation, Watanabe had no choice but to accept the order. The engineers were horrified

117

by the news. They had expected the completion date to be brought forward, but not by seven months.

During the height of the outfitting operation, 1,500 engineers and workers scurried around the Mukaijima outfitting dock, which was shielded on both sides by a high fence. The other exposed areas of the ship were once again hidden behind hemp screens.

Ten days after the launch honeycombed steel plates were lifted onto the deck of the ship. These were designed to prevent a shell or bomb from exploding inside the ship's smokestack.

Three days later, in the middle of the night, the ship was towed away from the outfitting quay for the removal of the launch rails, which were still attached to the ship's hull. Two days after that the ships electrical generators underwent their first tests.

The No. 2 slipway remained covered by hemp screens even after the launch. Watanabe was afraid that people would become suspicious if they saw the giant slipway empty. The hemp blinds that had been removed during the launch were quickly replaced. This did not stop various rumors from circulating around the city. Some people were sure that the slipway was now empty, while others believed that the ship had not yet been launched.

At about 9:30 P.M. on November 17 one end of the darkened No. 2 slipway suddenly blazed with light. The light soon took the orange tint of flame and spread to the hemp blinds on the neighboring No. 3 slipway. Soon the whole hemp cage was ablaze. Huge sections of the blinds began to fall to the slipway floor, spewing columns of sparks into the sky.

Thousands of citizens stood along the coast and in the hills, watching the spectacle. Many of them were certain that they could see the outline of a ship among the flames. The fire was extinguished at 11:00 P.M. The surface of the harbor, which had been turned orange by the blaze, returned to the black of the night sky.

Watanabe's team assembled at the No. 2 slipway soon after the fire had been put out. They discovered that the fire had been started by sparks from the welding on the *Kashihara-maru*, which was

118

being built on the No. 3 slipway. The ship that the citizens of Nagasaki had seen in the flames was the *Kashihara-maru*. The fire had destroyed almost half of the screens hanging over the No. 2 and 3 slipways, as well as seriously damaging the wooden scaffolding and supports around the *Kashihara-maru*.

Watanabe gave a nervous laugh. There had been two fires on the No. 2 slipway, but both had been small and easy to extinguish, leading the engineers to believe that the screens were fireproof. Now that they had seen how easily a fire had taken hold, they were amazed at their luck during the construction phase.

Watanabe stepped onto the flooded floor of the No. 2 slipway. Through the gaps between the hemp screens, he could see the stars in the night sky, and beneath them, the lights of the villages on the coast.

At the end of December workers fitted the aft bridge and finished the boat hangars. In June the bridge and the smokestack were installed. The vessel was finally beginning to look like a battleship.

The No. 1 bridge stood forty meters above the water, and over fifty meters from the bottom of the hull. The interior was divided into thirteen storeys, connected by a high-speed elevator. With the smokestack and most of the armor plating in place, all that remained was the mounting of the main and auxiliary guns, which were being ferried from Kure by the *Kashino*.

\* \* \*

In the summer of 1941 Germany and Italy declared war on the Soviet Union, and the Axis forces began their eastward advance. Meanwhile Great Britain and the United States had intensified their economic pressure on Japan by freezing all Japanese assets and imposing trade sanctions. The mood of the Japanese people was dark, and many believed that war with Britain and the United States was inevitable.

In late June a five-man Navy outfitting team, led by Captain

Kaoru Arima, arrived at the Nagasaki Shipyard. Arima, the new battleship's first commanding officer, had graduated from the advanced course of the Navy's Ordnance School and then attended the Naval Staff College. His brief was to evaluate the mechanical features of the No. 2 Battleship and determine whether or not these would be practical during combat. His team would also study the ship in order to determine how to train its first crew. Arima's arrival was a clear sign to the shipyard that the battleship would soon be ready for active duty.

The team's trip to Nagasaki was kept secret, and all its members left Tokyo in civilian clothes. The officers' names were struck from the Navy's active duty roster, and even once they were on site, they were forced to remain undercover. A fake sign was fitted to the door of their office to make it look like a civilian subcontractor.

At 8:00 P.M. on October 6 the *Kashino*, carrying the first of the nine 46-centimeter guns, pulled alongside the No. 2 Battleship. A 350-ton capacity derrick crane hoisted the huge gun and turret from the deck of the transport ship. The workers looking up at the massive piece of steel hanging in mid-air were astounded by its size: twenty-one meters long on a turret twelve meters in diameter.

When the gun had been lowered into position on deck, it was covered with a canvas cover. From that day on, the *Kashino* arrived in Nagasaki at regular intervals with the ordnance for the battleship.

\* \* \*

On October 18 Prime Minister Konoe's third cabinet resigned, making way for a new administration headed by General Hideki Tojo. An Imperial Conference held on September 6 had already decided that Japan would declare war on the United States and Britain sometime toward the end of the year. The Tojo administration continued diplomatic negotiations with Washington, while it prepared Japan for war.

Shortly after the change in administrations, the Navy ordered the shipyard to finish the outfitting of the No. 2 Battleship fifteen days ahead of schedule. Protesting that the request was impossible, Ogawa nevertheless agreed to push the completion date forward.

Japan and the U.S. were on the brink of war. On November 26 Secretary of State Cordell Hull sent an ultimatum to the Japanese government. The "Hull Note" called for a withdrawal of Japanese troops from China and French Indochina and denounced the puppet regime of Manchukuo. The Japanese government realized this was the last peaceful communication it would have with the United States.

On the morning of December 8 the citizens of Nagasaki were woken from their sleep by a special radio announcement: "Early this morning the Imperial Japanese armed forces began hostilities with the United States and Britain in the Pacific." The shrill voice of the announcer sounded panicked as he repeated the news.

As soon as shipyard executives heard the report, they ran from their homes to Watanabe's office. The executives and naval supervisors then gathered in the shipyard president's office. Ogawa and Shimamoto addressed the group, urging them to complete the outfitting as soon as possible, with Shimamoto stressing the great importance of the No. 2 Battleship to the Navy.

Two days after the raid on Pearl Harbor had been announced, a squadron of Japanese planes sank Britain's HMS *Prince of Wales* and HMS *Repulse* off the Malaysian Coast. Meanwhile, the Japanese Army had taken the islands of Guam and Luzon in the Philippines.

On December 16 Watanabe received news from the Kure Arsenal that all work had been completed on the No. 1 Battleship. Construction had begun on November 4, 1937, exactly four years and one month before. The battleship had been given the name *Yamato* and immediately sent to the First Squadron of the Combined Fleet.

Watanabe and Koga had mixed feelings about the completion of the *Yamato* at Kure. The fact that construction of the *Yamato* had

121

started only four months before the No. 2 Battleship at Nagasaki meant that the final outfitting work should have been completed at Nagasaki by the coming March. The shipyard was actually planning to complete the No. 2 Battleship almost four months after that, however, in July.

The No. 2 Battleship had taken longer to build because while the arsenal had all of the equipment necessary for the construction of a modern battleship, most of the equipment and materials for the No. 2 Battleship had to be shipped to Nagasaki from Kure. Another consideration was the technical advantage of building a battleship on a dry dock rather than on a slipway when it came to launching the huge vessel. Last but not least, the shipyard had been forced to preserve the secrecy of the project from a city located directly above it. It would seem natural that the completion of the No. 2 Battleship would take at least four months longer than the No. 1 Battleship, but the Navy would not hear of any such excuses.

For Watanabe and Koga, the string of victories announced on the radio after December 8 was almost painful. Manila fell on January 2, 1942. On the thirteenth a parachute squadron landed in Menado. On the twenty-third Japanese troops landed on Rabaul, and on the thirty-first they took Johore Baharu. Between February and early March the Japanese scored three victories at sea against the Allies in the battles of the Java Sea, Surabaya, and Batavia.

Arima's second in command, Captain Sadakata, had already asked the Yokosuka Naval Station and the Navy Ministry to send a crew for the No. 2 Battleship. He thought that if the crewmen saw the outfitting process, they would learn how to operate the ship far more quickly and have the new vessel almost immediately ready for battle. The trainees arrived in Nagasaki a few at a time, and by March fifty officers and 1,000 petty officers and seamen were visiting the shipyard regularly.

Arima took his trainees to watch practice drills with the battleship *Yamato* in the Seto Inland Sea, and asked the crew of the *Yamato* if there were any problems with the design of the new ship.

Arima collected dozens of small complaints from the *Yamato*'s crew, but the suggestions for improvements included only minor items. The outfitting team realized that if it made requests for fundamental changes, it would be faced with aggressive opposition from the shipyard. Its real objective was to have the battleship completed as quickly as possible.

Despite Arima's efforts to reach a compromise, however, the shipyard was soon confronted with a request for important changes and improvements. Watanabe and Koga had expected such an order from the Bureau of Naval Construction, but when it came it included a request from the General Staff of the Combined Fleet for major revisions in the No. 2 battleship's flagship facilities.

A heated argument had taken place between the Naval General Staff and the Bureau of Naval Construction over the outfitting of the *Yamato*. In the end only a few minor revisions had been made to the *Yamato* because it was near completion. But the Naval General Staff was not going to be so easily swayed from getting its way with the No. 2 Battleship, which was still four months away from completion.

Watanabe winced when he saw the order. Two months before, the Bureau of Naval Construction had requested that he move up the original ship's completion date of July 15 by more than one month to June 10. The revisions included the expansion of the flagship and bridge facilities and the reinforcement of the armor covering the auxiliary gun turrets. The main guns on the *Mogami*-class battle cruisers had been shifted without modifications to the No. 1 and No. 2 battleships to be used as auxiliary guns. Arima insisted that the armor on the turrets was insufficient for a battleship.

Watanabe thought that the modifications asked for by the Bureau of Naval Construction would make a completion date of June 10 impossible. He and Koga contacted the Navy immediately and made their opinions clear concerning the revisions and their effect on the delivery date. In the end the Navy agreed to push the completion date back almost two months to August 5.

Workers began the massive revision program immediately. The revisions alone would cost two million yen, the price of building a destroyer in 1942.

* * *

At 4:20 P.M. on April 18 the air-raid sirens sounded in Nagasaki for the first time. Sixteen B-25s from the carrier *Hornet* had raided Tokyo, Nagoya, and several other targets in western Japan. Nagasaki had not been bombed, but Yokosuka had sustained light damage.

Soon after the raid the Navy informed Watanabe that construction on the No. 3 and No. 4 battleships had been halted, because the ships would take too long to build to be of practical use in the war. But Watanabe was well aware that the decision represented a major shift in naval thinking, which was moving away from the bigger is better theory for battleships and ordnance to strengthening air power. The Doolittle Raid had done little physical damage, but it had alerted the Navy to the enormous potential of carrier-borne aircraft.

During the final stages of the outfitting revisions, the crew reached almost 1,500 men. The trainees were given explanations about the construction and various features of the ship by the engineers who had built it. For them the No. 2 Battleship was different from any other warship they had been assigned to, and not just because of its enormous size; the interior of the ship was divided up into innumerable compartments and packed with much more machinery and equipment than they had ever seen on a battleship. Once inside the hull, it was impossible to tell fore from aft, and the trainees often got lost. Fortunately, the ship was equipped with 491 direct telephones and 461 speaking tubes, besides an operator-run telephone system.

In most battleships ventilation was extremely poor, and the heat in summer was especially stifling. The No. 2 Battleship, however, was equipped with air-conditioning units, as well as 282 electric fans. The seamen's quarters were unusually spacious, with an average of 3.2 square meters of floor space per man—over three times as much space as in a destroyer. Each man slept in a bunk rather than a hammock. The captain's quarters were more luxurious than the best suite of a luxury hotel, with a reception room, separate living quarters, a large bathroom, and a captain's galley.

The outfitting revisions were completed in early May. With almost all of the No. 2 Battleship operational, the only work left was the final stage of outfitting at Kure. The battleship would sail to the arsenal under its own power. With only three months left before the battleship had to be delivered to the Navy, the shipyard did not have time to test the engines at sea before the trip. Instead, Watanabe chose a night in May to test the engines with the ship in dock.

Construction work on the No. 2 Battleship ended on May 16, 1942, and workers began preparing the vessel for its journey to Kure. It took three days to clean the ship's interior and provision it with fuel, water, and stores. Anticipating the possibility of an attack from enemy aircraft, the anti-aircraft guns and machine guns were loaded with live ammunition.

On May 19 all the shields around the No. 2 Battleship were removed, and the vessel was towed away from the Mukaijima outfitting dock and anchored at a buoy in the harbor. The following morning a mixed Navy and shipyard crew boarded the ship. At 3:05 P.M. the battleship was towed by a tugboat toward the mouth of Nagasaki Harbor. Policemen lined the coast, and the city streets were silent and abandoned.

At 4:10 P.M. the battleship sailed out of Nagasaki Harbor, and the lines connecting it to the tugboat were released. Four years and two months after workers had first started construction, the No. 2 Battleship was at sea. The engines started up, the propellers began to rotate, and slowly the battleship began moving under its own power. The tugboat faded into the distance, and in its place two destroyers appeared in front of the battleship. Two seaplanes from the

Sasebo Naval Station patroled the skies overhead.

Acting ship's captain Eiji Nagatsuma from the Nagasaki Shipyard's External Affairs Department took the battleship from eighteen to twenty knots, setting a course that would take the ship around the Osumi Peninsula in order to avoid the narrow Kanmon Strait.

The red glimmer of the evening sun on the sea finally faded as night fell. Shortly after midnight the battleship passed around the Osumi Peninsula. It reached the Hyuga Shallows at dawn, continuing its journey northward along the east coast of Kyushu. Sailing into Hiroshima Bay by way of Kurahashi Island, the No. 2 Battleship entered Kure harbor at about 4:00 P.M. on May 21.

Soon after the battleship had been towed into a dock in the arsenal, barnacles, shellfish, and seaweed were removed from the bottom of the hull and a special paint was applied. Two weeks later, when the battleship left the dock, its anti-aircraft guns and machine guns were loaded with ammunition and the testing of its armaments began.

On June 18 the battleship left Kure Harbor at 7 A.M. with a crew of 3,200 Navy and shipyard personnel for its official sea trials in the Iyo Sea.

The ship's unique pumping system, which controlled over 1,147 compartments throughout the ship's hull, underwent rigorous testing. If a torpedo hit the battleship below the waterline, causing it to list as water flooded into the hull, the crew could flood compartments on the opposite side of the hull to balance it. If the damage was not too severe, water could also be pumped out of the flooded portion of the hull.

About one month later, after more machine guns had been added, the main guns were tested at sea. Engineers placed gauges on the battleship's deck to measure the blast pressure caused by the firing of the main guns.

A buzzer rang immediately before the first test firing. The crew went below decks. The moving target, which was 38,000 meters away, could just be seen the horizon.

On the battleship's bridge, Navy observers stood with shipyard executives, staring at the distant target. They had all been warned to stop up their ears and hold onto a stationary object.

The "fire" signal lit up. The men on the bridge were suddenly overwhelmed by the shock wave, as if their guts had suddenly been thrust upwards into their throats. Taking a tighter grip, they stared at the target ship. The smoke from the guns drifted across their field of vision, but there was still no change in the target. Minutes seemed to pass as everyone waited. Finally they saw the ocean foam up just in front of the target. Just as the foam seemed about to subside, a huge pillar of water erupted from the water's surface. When it finally reached its maximum height, it was half as tall as the mountains behind it.

The precision of the main guns was beyond everyone's expectations. Nine test firings were held that day before the ship returned to port. The instruments on the deck showed that anyone standing topside when the guns were fired would be seriously injured by the blast pressure. The guinea pigs that had been placed in cages on deck had been literally blown apart.

At the end of July Shimamoto reported to the Bureau of Naval Construction that all features and armaments on the No. 2 Battleship were in order, and that the ship was ready to be handed over to the Navy for use in the fleet.

\* \* \*

That same month former Nagasaki Shipyard president Kyosuke Tamai traveled from Mitsubishi head office to the shipyard. Tamai paid his respects to Ogawa and asked, "What is the name of the No. 2 Battleship?"

Ogawa turned to Watanabe and Koga, who were also present. Watanabe grinned slightly, but said nothing. He quickly scrawled something on a scrap of paper with a pencil. After showing it to Tamai, he crumpled up the paper and burnt it in an ashtray.

Tamai remained silent and simply nodded. So it's *Musashi*, he said to himself. It lacked the power of *Yamato*, but it suggested the autumn storms of the Musashino Plain. As he repeated the name over and over to himself, he began to think that it was probably the best name for the No. 2 Battleship.

"No one else knows?" Tamai asked, staring at Watanabe. "About three or four people, I think, but I'm not really sure," Watanabe answered.

"Aren't you going to announce the name at the commissioning ceremony?" Tamai asked.

"The name will be announced to the crew once the ceremony is over, and the ship has left port," Watanabe answered.

"About that No. 3 battleship that was being constructed in Yokosuka," Tamai said, "I've heard that they decided to convert it into an aircraft carrier."

Ogawa and the others stared at Tamai.

The No. 4 Battleship under construction at Kure had been dismantled, and the steel plates piled in a warehouse. The news that the No. 3 Battleship was being rebuilt as an aircraft carrier was a clear signal that the Navy was placing less and less importance on battleships.

Tamai frowned and said, "It seems that our defeat at Midway was the reason for the decision."

Watanabe remembered walking into the Navy outfitters' office two months before. Looking around he realized that all of the men in the room seemed strangely confused, standing silently with their arms folded. Watanabe, thinking he had walked into something he should not have, immediately left the room. He found out later that the officers had just received news of the disastrous defeat at Midway.

A task force of aircraft carriers, commanded by Vice Admiral Nagumo and directed by commander-in-chief of the Combined Fleet, Isoroku Yamamoto, had made an aerial attack on the U.S. base on Midway just before dawn on June 5. Yamamoto decided to make a second attack on the base, and as the men were exchanging the torpedoes on the aircraft with surface bombs, they were surprised by a small enemy squadron of about thirty planes. The Americans sank four aircraft carriers in the attack. The air superiority that Japan had demonstrated in its attacks on Pearl Harbor and Malaysia was used against it at Midway.

Watanabe realized that battleships the size of the *Yamato* and the *Musashi* would never again be built anywhere in the world. With the vast improvements in aircraft technology, battles between warships were being replaced by aerial attacks against naval vessels. But Watanabe still believed that he *Musashi* would not sink under normal attack. It was not a ship but a mobile fortified island. Watanabe felt as if he almost could not bear to part with this fortress, which he had seen through from construction to launch.

On the morning of August 5 the commissioning ceremony for the No. 2 Battleship was held in Kure. The ceremony began on the main deck near the bow. Lined up on the left were Shimamoto and his men, in the center was Captain Arima and his outfitting team, and on the right Ogawa with about 100 shipyard employees.

Arima had suggested that a priest from the Hikawa Shrine in Saitama Prefecture, the modern name of Musashi Province, preside over the Shinto rites. Afterwards Ogawa officially handed over the ship to the Navy.

The ceremony then shifted to the stern, where the naval ensign was raised, as crewmen and shipyard workers stood to attention. Arima and the other Navy officers then shook hands with every single shipyard employee present and thanked them for a difficult job well done.

Ogawa and his men left the ship by motor launch. The civilian workers who had spent so much time building the *Musashi* would, from that day forth, never have the chance to board it again. As the launch pulled away from the battleship, the shipyard personnel could see Arima and the other Navy men waving at them from the main deck. When the workers were back ashore, they stared for a long time at the vast ship, still tied to a buoy in the harbor.

129

"Well, I guess it's time to go," one of them said. The workers all hung their heads and followed Ogawa through the busy arsenal to the front gate. They were now just shipyard employees, with no more connection to the No. 2 Battleship than any other civilian in Japan.

# 20
# Preparing For Battle

**Summer 1942**

It had taken more than a year to outfit the No. 2 Battleship in Nagasaki and test it at Kure and in the Seto Inland Sea. On August 5, 1942, the day of its commissioning, the *Musashi* was incorporated into the First Squadron of the First Fleet.

On that same day the ship's name was officially recorded for the first time in the log. The crew, however, knew only the areas of the battleship that were immediately related to their jobs. The specifications of the vessel, such as its weight and length, remained strictly secret.

Basic statistics, which were usually written near the bow for easy reference, were not recorded using the normal method. The vessel's name was written in a Japanese numeric code in the form of a fraction—6/34—which, when read from numerator to denominator, could be read as *Mu-sa-shi* (6-3-4), a colloquial Japanese pronunciation of the three numbers. In order to hide the number of crew members on board, the Navy added 100 to each division number on the ship, with the first division designated as 101.

After leaving the Kure Arsenal, the *Musashi* anchored for a short time at Hashirajima in Kure Harbor. The sea around Hashirajima was enclosed by islands, so the Navy was confident the battleship could not be spotted from the mainland.

One day Captain Arima addressed the entire crew assembled on the foredeck. "This battleship is unsinkable," he began. "You must never forget that it is a great privilege to serve on this ship. The battleship *Yamato* is already on active duty. The battleship *Musashi* must not be outshone by the *Yamato*. It must become the Imperial Navy's foremost warship. All of you must undergo training to operate this ship above and beyond the call of duty. As of this moment, I want you all to think of every day as a day at war."

From that day forth the crew began a painstaking training program in the Iyo Sea, using Hashirajima as their base of operations. Intense repetitive training was necessary for the crew to become accustomed to the complex equipment on the ship. The Navy's careful choice of petty officers and seamen paid off with unusually good performances during training exercises.

Early in 1943 the *Musashi* ended four months of exercises and joined the Combined Fleet as a fighting ship. The Japanese were losing the battle for the Solomon Islands, and it seemed almost certain that the U.S. would take Guadalcanal.

On January 18 the *Musashi* weighed anchor at Hashirajima, and with an escort of three destroyers, sailed out into the Pacific Ocean. The *Musashi*'s destination was a point 2,100 nautical miles southsoutheast—the Truk Islands—where the Combined Fleet was stationed.

Storms and high waves during the journey jostled the destroyers accompanying the *Musashi*, but the battleship remained completely unaffected by the choppy water. The white foam of the waves simply splashed off its sides. The crew was cheerful. The *Musashi* was larger by far than any other vessel in their experience. The accompanying destroyers took turns racing ahead of the battleship, then slowed their propellers to check sonar and see if any enemy submarines might be lurking below. No alerts were sounded, and the *Musashi* continued steadily on its course.

As the ships passed the Ogasawara Islands, three days after leaving Hashirajima, the sun grew noticeably stronger, and the captain ordered his crew to change into summer uniforms.

The crew got their first glimpse of the Truk Islands on the afternoon of their fifth day after leaving Hashirajima. They approached at low tide, when the sixty-kilometer coral reef was most visible against the white foam of the breakers. Dark green islands, large and small, dotted the lagoon.

The *Musashi* entered the reef from the north. Several ships of the Combined Fleet were docked around one of the islands. The crew of the *Musashi* recognized the battleships *Hyuga*, *Ise*, and *Nagato*, in addition to several aircraft carriers, destroyers, and battle cruisers.

As the *Musashi* circled the island, the crew caught sight of a battleship so huge, most could not identify it. It was a vessel of such monstrous proportions that it seemed to be almost as high as the peaks of the island mountains towering behind it. This was the *Yamato*, and the crew of the *Musashi* was suddenly filled with pride when they realized they were aboard a ship of exactly the same scale and design.

After anchoring next to the *Yamato*, small launches were lowered from the *Musashi*'s stern. These carried Captain Arima and his officers across the tranquil waters of the lagoon toward the *Musashi*'s twin.

News quickly spread that the Combined Fleet was planning to transfer flagship status from the *Yamato* to the *Musashi*. The crew of the *Musashi* was enthusiastic. To be a crewman of the fleet's flagship was the highest honor for a seaman. The designation also meant that the commander-in-chief, Admiral Isoroku Yamamoto, would be stationed on board.

The fleet, of course, had decided to make the *Musashi* the new flagship because it had been specially designed for that purpose. In fact, the extra outfitting had delayed its completion by almost two months.

While the crew was still adjusting to its new status, Arima and his officers were shocked by another piece of news: The Americans had taken Guadalcanal. Losses in combat totaled 15,000 men, and 4,500 more had died of sickness and starvation before Japanese forces had finally surrendered. The Navy had lost 853 fighter planes, as well as several vessels. Japanese forces were already small in comparison to the Americans, and the losses at Guadalcanal were an unexpected blow.

After occupying Guadalcanal, U.S. troops put all of their efforts into building an airstrip on the island. Still, no enemy planes had been sighted over Truk.

On February 11 the entire crew of the *Musashi* turned out on deck to welcome Admiral Yamamoto. A military band played the *Shokanreishiki* as the C-in-C's flag was lowered from the *Yamato*'s mast.

The C-in-C's launch was lowered from the gunwales of the *Yamato* and made its way slowly toward the *Musashi*. In a few short minutes the crew of the *Musashi* heard the sound of footsteps on the rungs of the ladder up from the launch. A group of staff officers appeared, followed by the deeply tanned Yamamoto. The moment he stepped on the main deck, his flag was unfurled on the mast. He reviewed the ship's company and crossed the main deck to his quarters.

The *Musashi* entered yet another phase of intense training exercises while it was stationed at Truk, concentrating on the ship's ordnance. The atmosphere on the island remained peaceful, and the crew of the *Musashi* was far from preoccupied with thoughts of war. South Pacific squalls would move into the lagoon once or twice a day. A characteristically cool breeze swept over the ship, and crew members would look out at the horizon for the regular black mass of fast-approaching rain clouds.

"Squall!" a lookout would shout, and crew members who were on deck would run for soap, take off their clothes, and jump out into the rain, washing off the day's sweat and cleaning their uniforms. The soapy water would wash over the battleship deck. In a few short minutes the rain would pass and the sun would again beat down on the steel hull. The green of the palm trees on the island coast seemed even deeper under the intense afternoon sunlight after a squall.

There was almost no contact between the C-in-C and members

of the crew, but they would snap to attention and salute whenever he came into sight. No matter how hot it became on deck, Yamamoto never wore a tropical uniform. Instead, he always appeared in a neatly pressed white dress uniform.

In his free time, Yamamoto would occasionally join members of his staff for a game of ring toss on deck. A rumor circulated among the crew that Yamamoto and his officers were betting glasses of beer on the matches. Yamamoto always won, and the officers grinned nervously during the competition.

Yamamoto was certain to leave his quarters to see off a ship or fighter squadron departing for battle. The ships or aircraft would come close to the *Musashi*, and the C-in-C would wave his cap in the air as they passed.

Two months went by, and still the *Musashi* rode at anchor. On rare occasions, the anti-torpedo net would be removed from around the hull and the *Musashi* would join the *Yamato* in drills inside the reef.

With the capture of Guadalcanal, the Americans were able to retake New Guinea. With Japanese troops on the defensive, the Americans concentrated their attacks on Lae and Salamaua. In the subsequent battle, Japan lost almost 4,000 troops, four destroyers, and thirty fighters.

# 21
## An Imperial Visit

**Spring 1943**

After the fall of Guadalcanal the U.S. offensive was unstoppable, and Japanese forces all over the Pacific were on the retreat. Yet the *Musashi* and *Yamato* remained idle at the Truk anchorage. The crew of the *Musashi* underwent rigorous daily training, but months passed, and the ship was not sent to battle.

The Naval General Staff had decided that sending the two battleships out on minor missions would only risk damaging the vessels and revealing their existence to the United States. Instead, the Navy was waiting for a full-scale naval battle in the hopes of picking off enemy ships with the forty-six-centimeter guns on the *Yamato* and *Musashi*, at a distance that left the enemy craft still far out of firing range.

Another reason for waiting was the two battleships' ravenous appetite for fuel. With 6,300 tons of storage capacity each, the *Yamato* and the *Musashi* could sail 8,600 nautical miles at nineteen knots, but at their maximum speed of twenty-seven knots this dropped to 4,100 nautical miles. In a battle situation, the speed of the ships would be comparatively high, and the Navy reasoned that if they were dispatched on minor missions, they would be using fuel that might be needed for a larger battle.

Both the battleships avoided leaving the reef as a precaution against attack by enemy submarines; most of the drills were performed with both ships tied to their buoys.

The *Musashi* finally sprang into action on April 4. Shortly after dawn Yamamoto and several of his staff officers boarded two type

1 land-based attack planes. The aircraft took a southward route. On the *Musashi*, the remaining staff officers and Captain Arima waved them off from the deck. Only they knew the C-in-C was going to Rabaul to supervise an important offensive.

The outcome of the "I" battle, as the Japanese called it, was extremely favorable, which helped to lift the spirits of Captain Arima and the officers on the *Musashi*. The buoyant mood eventually spread to the rest of the crew.

The fleet at Rabaul sent a message to the *Musashi* saying that the engagement had ended on April 16, and that Yamamoto would go on an inspection tour of Bougainville and several other islands before returning to Truk on April 19.

But on the night of April 18 the staff officers on the *Musashi* were thrown into a state of confusion by a coded telegram that informed them that the two planes carrying the C-in-C and his staff and six escort fighters had been attacked by ten or more enemy aircraft over Bougainville Island at about 7:40 A.M. The No. 1 plane, carrying Yamamoto, had burst into flames and crashed into dense jungle about eleven nautical miles from the village of Buin on the west coast of the island. The No. 2 plane had crashed into the sea south of the island, and by the time the *Musashi* received the telegram, two of the officers had been rescued from the aircraft. On the evening of April 20 rescuers announced that there were no survivors from the No. 1 plane.

Yamamoto's staff officers were sworn to keep the C-in-C's death secret, but because Captain Arima and the other captains at Truk were expecting Yamamoto to return on the nineteenth, the Naval General Staff was forced to call a meeting of all commanding officers to inform them of Yamamoto's death and order them not to make the information public.

In order to avoid chaos in the fleet, the Navy wasted no time appointing Admiral Kondo of the Second Fleet to the position of vice commander-in-chief of the Combined Fleet.

On the afternoon of April 23 Yamamoto's cremated remains

137

were brought from Rabaul to Truk by plane. They were set on a Buddhist altar in the *Musashi*'s war operations room. The C-in-C's quarters and the operations room were sealed off from the rest of the ship so that the crew would not find out about Yamamoto's death.

An aircraft carrying the new C-in-C of the Combined Fleet, Admiral Mineichi Koga, left the Yokosuka Naval Station on the morning of April 24 and arrived at Truk the next day at 4:30 P.M. Koga's appointment was kept a secret even within the Navy. His promotion was reported at the Meiji and Yasukuni shrines in Tokyo as "a dispatch of the commander of the Yokosuka Naval Station to the South Seas." The Navy Ministry cars that had gone to the shrines did not bear the official insignia of the ministry. On May 5 vice chief of the Naval General Staff Ito arrived at the base to offer incense at the altar where Yamamoto's ashes had been laid.

The crew of the *Musashi* began to suspect that something was wrong. Some of them had seen the injured staff officers rescued from the No. 2 plane, while others noticed the "No Entry" signs in the corridors near the C-in-C's quarters and the smell of incense coming from the area.

Immediately after Ito had returned to Tokyo, U.S. units launched a surprise attack on Japanese-held islands in the north Pacific. They began their offensive on Attu Island in the Aleutians, and by May 12 had landed at two locations in the region. Japanese units attempted to cut the U.S. supply route to the islands, but the situation looked bleak. The Naval General Staff ordered the few remaining Japanese troops to retreat and prepared the main portion of the Combined Fleet for battle. News spread that the *Musashi* would participate in the battle for the north Pacific, and on May 17 the *Musashi*, followed by the bulk of the Combined Fleet, sailed out of the reef on a northerly course.

On May 21 the *Musashi*'s second in command announced to the crew that Yamamoto had died, and that the *Musashi* was taking his ashes back to Japan. He added that Admiral Mineichi Koga had already taken over as C-in-C of the Combined Fleet.

An all-night vigil was held for Yamamoto. Only the sound of the ship's engines could be heard through the silence until early morning. When the fleet arrived at the mouth of Tokyo Bay, the *Musashi* took a separate course and anchored in the Kisarazu Shallows.

On the following morning a farewell service for the C-in-C was held on deck of the *Musashi*. Then a staff officer carried Yamamoto's remains onto the destroyer *Yugumo*. As the crew of the *Musashi* paid their last respects, the *Yugumo* pulled out away from the battleship and headed for the Yokosuka Naval Station.

\* \* \*

Arima, who had acted as captain of the *Musashi* since its outfitting in Nagasaki, was promoted to the rank of vice admiral and was replaced by Lieutenant Commander Keizo Komura. After the outbreak of war Komura had been captain of the battle cruiser *Chikuma* and later of the battleship *Fuso*. He had seen action during the attacks on Pearl Harbor and Midway, and in battles in the Indian Ocean and the South Pacific.

Komura's first act as the *Musashi*'s captain was to steer a course for Yokosuka Naval Station. Soon after the battleship had docked, it was unexpectedly given notice that it would be visited by Emperor Hirohito. The visit would, of course, be carried out secretly, under the guise of a tour of Yokosuka. The real reason for the visit was to show the emperor one of the Navy's proud new battleships and to boost the morale of the crew. All shore leave was cancelled, and the crew was given a thorough medical to check for contagious diseases.

On June 24 a small motor launch flying the imperial standard cut a straight course across Yokosuka Harbor toward the *Musashi*. As it approached, a military band on the ship's deck began playing the national anthem, and the imperial standard was unfurled on the mast. Accompanying the emperor were his younger brother, Prince

139

Takamatsu, the imperial household minister, the minister of home affairs, the Navy minister and other top military and government officials. The imperial party toured the ship for two hours, guided by Komura and his officers.

The *Musashi* was given a new coat of paint at Yokosuka and re-fuelled before setting off for Kure. At Kure, barnacles were scraped from the *Musashi*'s gunwales before it was reloaded with ammunition, torpedoes, fuel, and stores.

The *Musashi* once again set a course for Truk. A great deal had changed since the *Musashi*'s last visit six months before. The Americans had strengthened their Pacific carrier task forces and begun an all-out offensive over the entire region. They had built an air base in the Solomon Islands and landed on New Georgia Island. In the north Pacific, they had taken the islands of Kiska and Attu.

The route to the Truk base was no longer safe. Anti-submarine aircraft flew in front of the *Musashi* as it sailed south, the crew kept all lights extinguished to keep the vessel as invisible as possible, and the ship sailed in a zigzag pattern throughout the entire journey.

# 22
# Riders On the Storm

**Autumn 1943**

In October, one month after the *Musashi* returned to Truk, Italy unconditionally surrendered, and Germany was under siege from a combined Allied offensive. In the central Pacific, U.S. troops took the Gilbert Islands, the Marshalls, the Caroline Islands, and the Marianas. The offensive annihilated the 4,500-strong Japanese garrison on Tarawa and Makin, and the 3,000-man force on the Marshall Islands.

As the front approached Truk, the *Musashi* remained peacefully anchored inside the reef. The crew passed time comfortably in the air-conditioned hull, oblivious of the approaching war. Only the smaller ships left to fight—many of them never to return. Others came back heavily damaged. The crews of the smaller vessels began to complain that the *Musashi* was being treated like a protected jewel by the Navy: It possessed some of the strongest armaments in the fleet and yet had never been sent into battle.

The crew of the *Musashi* was required to perform only a set of physical exercises every morning and little else. They helped build an airfield on the main island, known as Harushima by the Japanese, and grew crops for the ship on Akushima Island, but tropical weeds made it almost impossible to harvest anything.

In mid-October the Combined Fleet, including the *Yamato* and the *Musashi*, left Truk. The Navy had received news that an enemy fleet was heading for Brown Island. Soon after the ships had sailed, however, it was discovered that this report was false. The fleet spent three nights anchored inside the island's reef, and then returned to

Truk. The mission had only succeeded in wasting precious fuel.

In November Captain Komura was promoted to the rank of vice admiral, and on December 6 was made the commander of the Third Fleet. He moved to the battleship *Oyodo*, flagship of the Third Fleet. He was replaced as captain of the *Musashi* by Lieutenant Commander Toyoji Asakura, a former instructor at the Navy's Torpedo Academy.

On December 25, 1943, the *Yamato* returned to Truk with light damage after being torpedoed by an enemy submarine. Although the damage was not severe, the attack meant that the U.S. Navy now knew the scale of the new battleships. U.S. naval intelligence had known for some time that the Japanese had launched new battleships from Kure and Nagasaki, but they had discovered little else about the vessels. Some intelligence reports said the new battleships had a displacement of 35,000 tons with sixteen-inch guns, while others claimed 40,000 tons with eighteen-inch guns.

Commander E.B. MacKinney of the submarine USS *Skate* was the first foreigner to see the *Yamato* just before he torpedoed it on December 25. One look was not sufficient to get an accurate picture of the new ship, and the details of the design remained unknown to the U.S. military until the occupation of Japan.

The *Yamato* remained at Truk for a short time before returning to Kure for repairs.

\* \* \*

In the first days of 1944 U.S. troops scorched the Marshall Islands with an impressive display of firepower, killing over 3,000 Japanese troops. The fall of the Marshall Islands put Truk, only 1,000 nautical miles to the west, on the front line of the Pacific War.

At the beginning of February two B-24s overflew Truk. The fleet took this to mean that the island would soon be bombed. The Japanese air force had been wiped out during the Solomon Islands offensive, and almost no planes remained to protect the skies around Truk. The Navy ordered all warships to leave the area immediately, and vessels were soon hurrying away from the reef.

One part of the fleet headed for Palau, Japan's largest remaining base in the Pacific and the other for Singapore. The *Musashi*, escorted by several destroyers, set a course for Yokosuka. Only a short time after its departure the fleet received word that Truk had been attacked by 568 aircraft launched from an enemy carrier force. Thirty-two tankers and cargo ships that had not made it out of the reef in time had been sunk, and four destroyers had sustained heavy damage.

The main force of the Japanese fleet had just escaped in time, but the Truk base had been completely destroyed. With the raid on Truk, the United States controlled over half the Pacific Ocean.

The *Musashi* returned to Yokosuka, but was immediately ordered to sail to Palau. It transported an army division and large quantities of guns, torpedoes, ammunition, fuel, foodstuffs, and a fleet of transport vehicles. Enemy submarines made the crossing to Palau too hazardous for merchant ships, so the Navy was forced to rely on the *Musashi* to supply the base.

The *Musashi* sailed past the Izu Islands south of Tokyo into a dangerous typhoon area. Gigantic waves washed over the bow of the battleship, but the storm had little effect on the *Musashi*'s speed as it continued on its southward course.

The *Musashi*'s escort of three destroyers, however, were violently buffeted by the typhoon. The officers on the bridge of the *Musashi* could see the propellers of the destroyers as they were tossed from the sea. The smaller ships signaled to the battleship that crewmen had been swept overboard and that their hulls were being damaged by the storm. They pleaded with the battleship to slow down, and it obliged by dropping its speed from eighteen to six knots, with only one of its four axles rotating.

The *Musashi* had three huge piles of supplies lashed down to its main deck: bombs near the bow, barrels of crude oil and gasoline a midships, and cargo trucks aft. The relentless pounding of the waves was slowly loosening the ropes. The captain, afraid that the bombs would explode and ignite the oil and gasoline, ordered his crew to throw them overboard.

The storm lasted for two days. Most of the cargo on the main deck had been lost, but the *Musashi*'s crew had developed an almost mystical faith in their ship. The *Musashi* had managed to plow through one of the worst storms any of them had ever experienced, without having to reduce its speed, except to accommodate its escort of destroyers.

"The *Musashi* is unsinkable," the crew would say. "If it sinks, Japan will sink with it. And if Japan falls, we should go down with it."

On February 29, 1944, the *Musashi* anchored in the reef of the Palau Islands. After the army units had disembarked, the crew unloaded the supplies that had survived the journey.

On Palau, the *Musashi* crewmen faced a lifestyle no more fulfilling than during their year on Truk. The reef in Palau was even smaller than the one at the Truk, and the *Musashi* was forced to remain tied to its buoy. The crew took turns going ashore to dig air-raid trenches.

Exactly one month after the *Musashi* arrived in Palau, it received a warning from the Naval General Staff that a large squadron of enemy planes was heading west from New Guinea. The C-in-C and his staff were thrown into a frenzy, and they decided to evacuate immediately, as they had at Truk. Admiral Koga called Captain Asakura to his quarters and warned him that an air attack was imminent.

"Take the *Musashi* out to sea," the admiral ordered. "The general staff will go ashore to direct the fleet. We expect the enemy planes to come in from the south-southeast. The fleet should sail 180 nautical miles northeast of the islands. When the enemy has gone, return to Palau, and the general staff will reboard the *Musashi*."

To leave the reef, the huge battleship was forced to navigate a tiny channel on the west side of the main island—an eight and a half kilometer stretch with a minimum width of 110 meters and a tricky ninety-degree bend. The *Musashi* could only navigate the channel at high tide.

With less than two hours to go before high tide, Asakura ordered the crew to prepare for an emergency departure. While the Admiral Koga and his staff were put ashore in lifeboats, the battleship lowered its flagship ensign and weighed anchor.

Due to the *Musashi*'s size, one turn of the rudder would change its direction after about one minute and forty seconds. At full speed, the battleship would travel 1.4 kilometers before any steering correction could take effect.

Before entering the reef, Chief Navigator Sadae Ikeda had carefully studied the ninety-degree bend in the channel. He drew charts of the battleship's entry, hoping to repeat the successful maneuver when it exited. Asakura was uneasy about the hurried departure from the narrow channel, but Ikeda stood behind him on the bridge and took him step by step through the complicated series of maneuvers. Once the *Musashi* had left the channel and steered into the open sea, the crew took their lookout positions, and the ship sailed north, zigzagging at twenty-one knots.

# 23
# Attack!

**Spring 1944**

Suddenly a warning announced the approach of enemy torpedoes to starboard.

A second announcement reverberated through the battleship: "Torpedoes approaching from port at 135 degrees. Sound battle stations!"

The *Musashi* began a wide turn to port, but the three torpedoes continued to close in from behind. The battleship turned about seven degrees to starboard, then veered back to its original course. The maneuver caused the torpedoes to starboard to miss the hull, but the torpedoes to port were still closing. They were swinging fifteen degrees to starboard and heading for the ship's stern, closing in at about 400 meters. The chief navigator decided to swing the battleship to starboard. This would improve the *Musashi*'s chances of avoiding the torpedoes, but if they did hit, they might severely damage the rudders.

As he watched the path of the torpedoes, the navigator was confident that they would swing past the port bow if the battleship continued on its present course. But the unusually slow speed of the torpedoes ruined his calculations. Japanese torpedoes traveled at more than forty-five knots, but the American torpedoes were closing in at only about thirty knots. They were lumbering slowly through the sea behind the battleship, heading straight for the port bow.

The torpedo hit the battleship just below the port-side anchor, throwing a fifteen-meter column of water into the air. The ship's hull shook slightly, and crew members on deck heard a deafening explosion, like the sound of the ship's main guns being fired. The crew below decks heard only what sounded like someone tapping on an iron frying pan. The crew at the bow near the site of impact were not even aware that the *Musashi* had been hit. They thought that perhaps another ship nearby had been hit by a torpedo.

The area of the hull that had been holed had relatively weak defenses, and the rupture let water into one of the hull's many watertight compartments. The ship's pumping system went into action, and a compartment on the opposite side of the ship was flooded to prevent the ship from listing.

Captain Asakura reported light damage to the fleet. "Stability unchanged. Cruising speed of twenty-six knots possible. No other damage beside the rupture on the port bow."

The C-in-C ordered the *Musashi* to return to Kure for repairs, and the battleship navigated the 1,800 nautical miles back to the arsenal at a steady pace of twenty-three knots.

On the dock at Kure, engineers reported that the torpedo had made a hole approximately five meters in diameter, about six meters below the waterline. The water had not gone beyond the compartment where the torpedo had hit. About 2,000 tons of water had flooded into the hull through the hole.

As the water was pumped out of the hull, the bodies of seven seamen killed by the explosion flowed out of the hole with the sea water. Their bodies had turned white with decay during the journey back.

The damage to the hull was quickly repaired, and the ship used the time to improve its anti-aircraft armaments. The No. 2 and No. 3 auxiliary gun turrets were removed, and ninety-one twenty-five-millimeter machine guns were installed in their place. From afar, the battleship's deck looked like a mound of needles. As the Japanese Navy was anxious to catch up with U.S. radar capabilities, they also added four additional radar devices to the one already on board.

While the repairs and modifications were still under way, the crew was shocked by news that the C-in-C of the Combined Fleet, Admiral Koga had been killed. The C-in-C had been flying from Palau to a new base on Dabau with his staff in a squadron of fighter planes when they had encountered a storm. Koga's plane had gone down. He was the second C-in-C to die after leaving the *Musashi*, which gave rise to a superstition among the crew that the battleship was jinxed.

After a month in Kure the *Musashi* tested its machine guns in Saeki Bay. The ship's veteran crew also took the time to train new crewmen from the second volunteer corps and the youth corps. During the exercises the *Musashi* received an urgent order from the new C-in-C, Admiral Soemu Toyoda, to join the Combined Fleet for an offensive codenamed Operation "A."

U.S. forces had now spread over the entire Pacific region. The Combined Fleet, which had been avoiding direct contact with the U.S. Navy, decided that the time had come for a decisive confrontation. The *Musashi* immediately set off from Saeki Bay, heading south toward Borneo, where the vessels of the Combined Fleet had converged from all over the Pacific.

The Third Fleet, commanded by Vice Admiral Jisaburo Ozawa, consisted of nine aircraft carriers and sixteen destroyers. The Second Fleet, which would protect the third, was under the command of Vice Admiral Takeo Kurita and consisted of five battleships, including the *Yamato*, the *Musashi*, and the *Nagato*, ten heavy battle cruisers, and fifteen destroyers.

When reports reached the fleet that the Americans had begun landing on Biak Island, a Japanese base northwest of New Guinea, the *Yamato* and *Musashi* set a course for the island with an escort of destroyers and a land-based air patrol of 480 fighters. The strike force set off from Tawitawi on June 10 and anchored at Batjan to await further orders.

While the fleet was waiting, the Naval General Staff advised the *Musashi* that a large portion of the enemy fleet was heading for Saipan. It ordered the two battleships to break off the attack and return to the remainder of the Combined Fleet to participate in the "A" offensive.

The strike force wasted no time leaving Batjan and rejoining the rest of the fleet east of the Philippines, advancing to a point 500 nautical miles west of Saipan. Forty-two planes took off from Ozawa's carriers to locate enemy vessels. The enemy fleet was divided into four groups, with seven full-scale aircraft carriers, two smaller aircraft carriers, and eighty-one other vessels. It looked as if the U.S. Navy, too, had assembled all of its forces for this climactic showdown with the Japanese.

In June 1944 the U.S. Navy and Air Force was far superior to the Japanese, but Ozawa was determined to attack the Americans. On June 29, 246 fighters, bombers, and attack bombers took off from the Second Fleet as the first strike force. A second strike force of 100 planes took off immediately afterwards. Ozawa was planning to weaken the U.S. fleet from the air, and then send Kurita's battleships to face what was left.

The first strike force, however, was caught in dense clouds and could not locate the enemy. Instead, they were picked up by U.S. radar, ran directly into a waiting force of U.S. fighters, and were almost completely destroyed. The second strike force also covered a wide area looking for the enemy vessels without success. On their way to the Japanese base on Guam, they were surrounded by enemy fighters, and more than half of the squadron was destroyed.

The destruction of the two strike forces spelled doom for the "A" strategy. Ozawa, who had lost the greater part of his aircraft, notified the General Staff that the "A" offensive had been broken off. The fleet would be forced to retreat to avoid an enemy attack. The flagship of the Third Fleet, the state-of-the-art carrier *Taiho*, and the carrier *Shokaku* had already been hit by enemy torpedoes, and there was a danger they would be lost.

The Third Fleet was relentlessly attacked by aircraft launched from enemy carriers, which pursued it as it retreated. One by one, the aircraft carriers *Zuikaku*, *Junyo*, *Ryuho*, and *Chiyoda* were hit, and the carrier *Hiyo* was sunk by enemy torpedoes.

Kurita's fleet had sent out reconnaissance planes and actually managed to locate a squadron of enemy planes, flying 40,000 meters away off the coast of Borneo. The *Yamato* and *Musashi* aimed their forty-six-centimeter guns at the enemy squadron and fired continuously in a 400-meter arc, downing over twenty U.S. planes. The crew on the two battleships saw no signs of enemy fighters after the initial attack.

After the engagement, Kurita's fleet received a welcomed order to call off the attack and joined up with Ozawa's fleet heading back to Kure.

Two of the Japanese Navy's three full-scale carriers had been sunk, as well as one of its three auxiliary carriers, and 280 carrier-based aircraft had been lost. The *Musashi*, which had never before had the chance to confront the U.S. fleet, had only been teased into running around the Pacific and using up its fuel, and was now once again tied to a buoy in port.

During the ten days the fleet was at Kure, radar devices, which the Japanese had finally succeeded in mass-producing, were installed on each vessel. Surprise and night attacks, which had been a specialty of the Japanese Navy, were consistently foiled by U.S. radar, and the Americans always managed to strike first. The frustrated officers and crew welcomed the new devices with high expectations after the heavy losses they had sustained in their last attempted surprise attack. Additional twenty-five- and thirteen-millimeter-machine guns were also fitted to any ship that had room on its deck.

The fleet could not stay in Kure forever. Enemy submarines were sinking Japanese tankers in the Pacific, and had managed to almost completely cut off oil supplies from Southeast Asia. Japan's oil reserves were desperately low, and the longer the fleet remained in port, the greater the likelihood that it would never move again.

The Naval General Staff ordered the Combined Fleet to sail to the Lingga base near the Palembang oil fields for exercises. The fleet left Kure on July 8. On this voyage, too, the *Musashi* was used as a transport ship, loaded with supplies for the 3,000 troops fighting in Burma.

The Lingga base was about 130 nautical miles south of Singapore on the east coast of Sumatra. It was surrounded on all sides by small islands. Located on the equator, the base had almost no wind circulation and was stiflingly hot. Fuel supplies from the Palembang oil fields were plentiful, and the whole fleet participated in a series of mock battle sequences.

Ozawa's carrier fleet had been lost, and the Japanese Navy was forced to continue the war with only battleships and cruisers. Everyone knew fighting the Americans without aircraft was suicide, but the Navy decided the fleet might succeed with a night attack.

During intensive nighttime training, the crew of the *Musashi* discovered they were able to fire their guns easily at any target the radar detected. They were confident that in a night attack they would be able to avoid enemy aircraft.

On August 15 the *Musashi's* fourth captain, Toshihira Iguchi, took over from Asakura. Iguchi's arrival was welcomed by the *Musashi* and the entire fleet. He was known throughout the Navy as an ordnance expert and was the only hope for a fleet that could no longer rely on air power.

# 24
# Operation *Sho*

**Autumn 1944**

With the war situation worsening by the day, Imperial Headquarters ordered another pullback and began planning a defensive battle called Operation *Sho*, which would consist of four successive phases designed to prevent the enemy from landing in Japan. Phase one would be fought around the Philippines; phase two, near Taiwan; phase three, near the home islands; and phase four, near Hokkaido and Sakhalin. Japan's leaders believed the U.S. Navy would first attack the Philippines, and preparations for phase one were started immediately. Phase one of Operation *Sho* had four major components:

1) Land-based aircraft will locate enemy vessels and attack them with torpedoes. When the enemy comes into range, Japanese Army units will fire from shore.

2) The Combined Fleet will gather in Brunei Bay in northern Borneo and will begin its attack when the enemy comes into range.

3) If the enemy manages to land on the Philippines, Japanese forces will mount an all-out counterattack.

4) Ozawa's carrier fleet will draw the enemy's carrier strike forces and afterwards join Kurita's fleet.

The first item was totally unrealistic in concept. With Japanese air power destroyed, the few aircraft that remained would have virtually no effect on the approaching enemy fleet. It seemed that the Combined Fleet would be forced to sail into enemy waters to make up for the lack of air power.

Kurita and his officers were very nervous about the plan to attack the American fleet, and then turn around and attack the beach where enemy troops had landed. Before the fleet could get to the landing site, it would have to sail through a treacherous swamp of enemy aircraft and submarines. For the fleet to risk all this to attack the enemy's landing craft was a strategic absurdity. If the Americans had managed a landing, the transports offshore would be empty. In addition, the U.S. Navy would probably lay mines around the approaches to the landing site, and many Japanese ships would surely collide with them.

One of the officers stood up and strongly opposed the plan. Captain Iguchi, the new commander of the *Musashi*, stressed the importance of a decisive confrontation with the American fleet. Kurita, hearing more and more voices of dissent among his officers, feared that the disagreement might have an effect on morale. He finally stepped in to defend the plan.

"The war is in its last stages," Kurita said, raising his voice over the officers' arguments. "Imperial Headquarters has decided that the Navy is not strong enough to fight a decisive battle with the enemy. That is why, as a last resort, they have opted for a surprise attack. Once the order has been given, all we can do is proceed as planned."

Imperial Headquarters was right about the enemy's plan to attack the Philippines. On the morning of October 17, 1944, a Japanese observation post at the entrance of the Leyte Gulf spotted an enemy fleet consisting of two battleships, two aircraft carriers, and six destroyers. At 8:00 A.M. the station reported that the Americans had begun landing on the island. The General Staff initiated the first phase of Operation *Sho* and immediately ordered Kurita to take his ships into Brunei Bay.

If the United States retook the Philippines, Japan would lose its main source of natural resources in the South Pacific, and the Navy would not be able to prevent an invasion of the home islands.

Kurita ordered his command to prepare for the crossing to Borneo.

Kurita's First Fleet consisted of thirty-two vessels, including the *Yamato*, the *Musashi*, and the *Nagato*. A smaller Second Feet, consisting of seven ships, under Vice Admiral Nishimura, was sailing to Leyte Gulf by a different route.

Ozawa's decoy fleet was left with only eight vessels, including four aircraft carriers and two converted battleship-aircraft carriers. Almost all of the sixty-three remaining vessels in the Japanese Navy were participating in the operation.

At 1:00 A.M. on October 18 Japan began mobilizing its forces. Kurita and Nishimura's fleets left the Lingga base. By about noon on October 20 Kurita's vessels had all arrived in Brunei Bay, where the ships were to be refueled. When the fuel tankers failed to show up on schedule, the destroyers transferred their fuel to the battle cruisers, and the battle cruisers transferred theirs to the battleships. Two fuel tankers arrived the next morning, however, and spent the entire day and evening refueling the fleet.

The crews were kept busy preparing for battle, removing all flammable materials from the interior of the ships. Crewmen on the *Musashi* even scraped the paint off the walls, fearing it might spread fire through the ship. The corridors and compartments were soon a dull steel gray.

On the eve of the battle the lifeboats of all the ships in Kurita's fleet gathered around the flagship. After the officers of each ship had discussed the final details of the battle, they toasted victory with cold saké. The crew of the *Musashi* also took part in a saké drinking party to mark the upcoming battle. They knew that the Leyte operation was practically suicide, but their undying faith in the unsinkable *Musashi* convinced them they would survive.

The lights inside the *Musashi* had been turned off and silence enveloped the ship. The drunken crewmen went to sleep. Only the trainee seamen stayed awake in their bunks, listening to the steady hum of the tankers refueling the ship.

On the morning of October 22 a bugle announced the beginning of the first battle of Operation *Sho* on the sun-drenched deck of the

*Musashi*. The heavy rumble of the anchor being lifted was followed by the sound of the engines.

All of the vessels in the fleet took the same course out of Brunei Bay, the *Musashi* followed the *Yamato*. The crewmen had wrapped *hachimaki* headbands around their foreheads in preparation for battle.

Twelve kilometers out of the bay, the fleet broke into two squadrons and headed due north at a speed of eighteen knots. The *Musashi* was with the First Squadron, immediately behind the *Yamato*.

That afternoon a destroyer warned the *Musashi* that an enemy submarine had been spotted. A loudspeaker announced the beginning of the battle, and the nervous crew prepared for the fight. The submarine turned out to be nothing but a piece of driftwood. It seemed that the enemy was still unaware of the whereabouts of the fleet.

Clouds gathered in the sky at dusk. At 7:00 P.M. the fleet stopped zigzagging and proceeded on a straight course, dropping its speed to sixteen knots, until it arrived at the channel to Palawan Island in the Philippines.

Stars shone in the night sky. Only the sound of the ship's engines reverberated through the *Musashi*'s hull. There was no feeling of motion. The excited crew could only toss in their bunks. Sleep was impossible.

At 5:20 A.M. the flagship *Atago* picked up a clear signal from enemy submarines. It immediately sent a warning to the rest of the fleet. Kurita's ships had finally been detected by the enemy. Another transmission confirmed that several American submarines were on his tail.

It was just before sunrise, but the fleet resumed a zigzag pattern as ordered by the flagship. The crew of the *Musashi* was already up and awake, and early morning drills were being held on the main deck. Seamen took their stations at the ship's guns and rapidly went through the firing routine.

155

As the stars faded and dawn broke the crew could see the outline of Palawan Island to starboard. At 6:30 A.M. the warning bugle suddenly sounded, and an order for the crew to man battle stations blasted over the ship's loudspeakers. At the same time the *Musashi* suddenly swung to port.

As crewmen were trying to regain their footing from the violent lurch, they heard the dull sound of an explosion to port. Three huge columns of water erupted from of the sea in quick succession, temporarily blotting other ships from view.

"The *Atago* is hit!" a lookout shouted.

Almost immediately, another column of water erupted next to one of the ships immediately behind the *Atago*. The sound of the explosion ripped through the early morning air.

"It's the *Takao*!"

As the column of water behind the *Takao* fell slowly back into the sea, black smoke spouted from its hull. The *Takao's* oil tanks had exploded.

Destroyers moved toward the crippled *Atago* and *Takao* and began to lay depth charges. White circles of foam from the underwater blasts soon rose to the surface around the ships, and the continuous din of the explosions could be heard over the sea. The *Atago* was developing a very distinct list, and the *Takao* had come to a complete halt.

The *Musashi* continued on its zigzag course with the rest of the squadron. Twenty minutes later the *Atago's* list had become extreme, and its bow was completely submerged.

As the *Musashi's* crew watched the *Atago* disappear into the ocean, a deafening explosion erupted from the midsection of the heavy cruiser *Maya*, sailing in front of the *Musashi*. A single column of fire rose into the air, glowing eerily in the morning sky. A strange substance like bright red cellophane erupted out of the flame and scattered over the ocean and ship below. A massive rupture had opened in the center of the *Maya*, and it quickly sank into the flaming oil-stained waters.

156

The activity on the main deck of the *Musashi* was frenzied. It was believed Vice Admiral Kurita and his staff were aboard the sunken flagship *Atago*, and the loss of the C-in-C and his staff would paralyze the fleet for the battle supposedly yet to come. The general staff, however, had been safely removed from the *Atago* to the destroyer *Kishinami*. Kurita had already designated the *Yamato* as his new flagship.

Megaphones on the various destroyers announced that the crew of the *Atago* would be taken aboard the destroyers *Kishinami* and *Asashio*. The *Akishio* would take the crew of the *Maya*, and the *Asashio* and the *Naganami* would be assigned to take the crew of the crippled *Takao* back to Brunei.

The fleet managed to ward off any further attacks from enemy submarines. Palawan Island receded into the distance.

In the afternoon the weather took a turn for the worse, and the smaller destroyers began to toss violently on rough seas. The destroyer *Shimakaze* approached the *Musashi* to transfer 769 of the crew of the *Maya*. Every one of them was coated in oil, and many were seriously injured.

Kurita and his staff had moved to the *Yamato*, and the admiral's ensign had already been raised on the battleship's mast. The fleet reassembled and continued northward. At 11:20 P.M. it changed course, heading southeast toward the Mindoro Straits.

At that time Kurita received a long telegram from the Naval General Staff, warning him that the U.S. Navy knew that he was heading for the Mindoro Straits. There was a strong possibility that he would be attacked by both land- and carrier-based aircraft early the next morning. The Americans also had a large fleet of submarines waiting for him in San Bernardino and the Surigao Straits, and the General Staff suspected that the U.S. fleet would reach San Bernardino near the Leyte Gulf by the afternoon of October 24.

Morning came. The sky was dotted with small clouds, and the surface of the sea was still. The *Musashi* passed south of Mindoro and headed northeast for the Sibuyan Sea. At 7:30 A.M. the crew of the *Musashi* was ordered to take a quick breakfast, because the fleet would soon be entering enemy waters.

The fleet formed an anti-aircraft ring, with the smaller ships in a circle around the *Yamato* patrolling the skies for approaching aircraft.

# 25
# The Battle

October 24, 1944, 8:10 A.M.–12:30 P.M.

At 8:10 A.M. the sound of a bugle call suddenly pierced through the silence of the ship, and loudspeakers blared the order for all crew to go to battle stations. With *hachimaki* tied around their foreheads, the crew ran to their posts.

As the activity on the main deck died down, gunners stared intently at the sky and the sea for signs of the enemy. A lookout sighted three U.S. B-24s far off to the north, circling widely and hiding behind light cloud cover.

The Japanese fleet had no planes in the air to support it. The crew of the *Musashi* stared helplessly at the distant enemy planes, which were probably informing their ships of the Japanese fleet's movements. As soon as the enemy planes disappeared, the *Musashi*'s deck burst into a blur of activity.

A message arrived from Kurita on the *Yamato*: "Enemy attackers are approaching. Trust in the gods and give it your best."

The captain of the *Musashi* relayed the message to his crew and the officers spurred their men on, sternly repeating the important points they were supposed to remember once the battle started. The crew of the destroyer *Maya* asked to be put to work and were soon assigned as extra crewmen at various battle stations.

At 10:00 A.M. the *Musashi*'s radar picked up enemy aircraft approaching from the east.

"Man anti-aircraft guns," blasted over the loudspeakers.

The guns and the 100-odd machine guns on the *Musashi*'s deck were aimed at the eastern sky. All of the hatches and air ducts had been shut tight to form a watertight partition between the main and lower decks. An eerie silence fell over the ship.

"Attack planes on the horizon, ninety degrees to starboard," a lookout shouted.

A huge squadron of enemy aircraft, shining like tiny metal shavings in the sky, appeared on the horizon. The light from the glittering metal grew in intensity as the planes approached.

The order was given to fire the main guns. Violent spasms shook the ship, and crewmen fought to keep their balance. The other ships in the fleet had also begun firing in the direction of the enemy squadron. The crew of the *Musashi*'s main deck could see sparks flying from the gleaming aircraft in the distance.

The main guns, which were unable to fire at aircraft at close range, stopped firing, and the auxiliary guns and anti-aircraft guns took over, followed by the machine guns. The deck was filled with a cacophony of gunfire. The anti-aircraft guns and machine guns swung around in furious, uncoordinated sweeps, a constant flow of gunfire spewing from their barrels. A multicolored light show of bullet tracks crisscrossed the sky overhead, and acrid black smoke spread over the deck.

An enemy fighter cut through the smoke over the *Musashi* at astounding speed, its metallic underside gleaming like the belly of a fish, trailing a long stream of transparent flame as it plummeted past the *Musashi* into the ocean. Other aircraft exploded immediately overhead.

It seemed the fighters were concentrating their attack on the *Yamato* and the *Musashi*. Columns of water exploded around the *Yamato* as the enemy fighters closed in around the two battleships. The aircraft made a high-pitched sound as they dive bombed toward the *Musashi*'s deck.

The *Musashi*'s machine guns divided into two groups and fired on the planes, but the U.S. squadron immediately broke off and retreated in the opposite direction, skimming over the surface of the water. Almost immediately, explosions drove large columns of

160

water up along either side of the *Musashi*, and a strange metallic sound resounded from the lid of the No. 1 gun turret. A one-meter circle of paint had been stripped off the turret's armor plate as a bomb dropped from an enemy aircraft bounced off it and into the sea.

The machine gunners continued to direct fire at the fighters overhead, until they noticed three attack bombers hugging the ocean and closing in from the starboard side. By the time they had seen the bombers, the planes had already released their torpedoes.

Foam rose from the ocean surface as the torpedoes cut into the water, heading straight for the *Musashi*. Two of the torpedoes whizzed past the hull, but the third slammed into the center of the starboard side. The explosion sounded throughout the ship, and a column of water rose along its side, sending a roaring wave over the main deck. Crewmen had to hold onto stationary objects to avoid being washed overboard.

Although it was not obvious to the gunners on the main deck, the ship was listing to starboard. Water was flooding in through the hole made by the torpedo. The rivets in the walls of the seventh and eleventh holds began to loosen, and water leaked through. The battleship was listing five degrees to starboard, but the pumping system was soon able to reduce the list to three degrees.

The enemy aircraft disappeared from sight, and all firing ceased. The crew stood paralyzed, while a relentless beating and ringing filled their ears. Their eyes were blurred from the smoke. The chief of the No.1 machine-gun squad had been killed by fire from an enemy fighter; other gunners had had their limbs blown off by explosions.

Crewmen emerged from hatches in the ship's fore and midsections to take the wounded to the infirmary. The *Musashi* reported to the *Yamato* that it had been hit on the starboard side by a torpedo. The damage was only a scratch for a ship the size of the *Musashi*, and it continued to sail at twenty-four knots. The jolt from the torpedo, however, had damaged the directional system of one of the main gun turrets, making it impossible to fire both guns simultaneously.

Everyone knew the enemy aircraft would return. The galleys on the *Musashi* passed out lunches to the men, but most were too busy checking equipment to eat.

At 11:40 A.M. the Musashi's radar picked up another squadron of enemy planes. The *Musashi* began to make a wider zigzag pattern as it continued along its course. The only sound was that of the choppy sea against the sides of the ship, and a tense silence again fell over the main deck.

At 12:03 A.M. a lookout announced, "Enemy squadron to starboard !"

The metallic gleam of a squadron much larger than that of the previous attack shone on the horizon. The main guns began firing alternately, and the air pressure on the ship rose and fell as they took their turns.

As the enemy planes approached, the crew realized they were heading outside the main circle of the fleet and were specifically aiming at the *Musashi*. The auxiliary guns fired, and the anti-aircraft guns roared. The machine guns were firing full-force. The ocean surface boiled where the bullets fell. One of the enemy planes dived and released torpedoes that slithered away from the aircraft, leaving thin tracks of foam behind them.

A line of six bombers flew low along the ocean surface and launched their torpedoes. The *Musashi* swung to port. One of the torpedoes raced past the ship's bow and two missed the stern, but the remaining three collided almost simultaneously on the port side. An enormous explosion shook the battleship, and a wave of water washed over the main deck. The force of the explosion threw seamen off their feet on the lower decks. Water gushed through holes in the hull and quickly flooded the No. 2 pumping room. The *Musashi* again listed five degrees to port.

The deck was submerged by huge surges of seawater created by the explosion. As the ship listed on its zigzag course, water rolled

162

off the deck like a giant waterfall. The machine guns were firing into the air in all directions. Despite the damage, the crew managed to keep the ship going at full capacity. Like an injured animal that strikes out when cornered, the great ship fought back with renewed force.

A reverberating clanging noise could be heard periodically as bombs bounced off the thick steel skin of the battleship. Six enemy bombers descended and scored two direct hits with 250-kilogram bombs on the port side. One hit the crew quarters, killing everyone inside. The shock wave and shrapnel from the blast injured many of the other crewmen in the immediate area.

A second bomb hit the front of the No. 4 anti-aircraft gun. It penetrated the upper deck and the main deck and exploded on the mid-deck. All of the crew in the munitions chamber were killed by the blast.

The explosion of the second bomb caused a fire in the No. 2 engine room and damaged one of the port-side axles. The *Musashi* was left with three of its four propellers operative.

After the second enemy attack, Captain Iguchi reported the damage to Vice Admiral Kurita on the *Yamato*. "Hit by three torpedoes and two bombs."

An ordinary battleship would have sunk after sustaining such heavy damage, but, once again, the *Musashi* used its pumping system to bring the five-degree list down to one degree. With no loss in speed, it continued to keep pace with the rest of the squadron.

The main and lower decks of the *Musashi* were strewn with bodies. The dead were left where they were, and a continuous stream of wounded was carried to the ship's infirmaries, where blood soaked the floors. The ship's doctors and paramedics were busy giving first aid to as many wounded as possible.

A seaman stood in the middle of the infirmary with a dripping red tourniquet hanging from the stump where his arm had been blown off. Next to him another sailor with a piece of shrapnel still embedded in his face sat in a chair. When a doctor approached to treat them, they insisted they were all right and told him to see to the other men first.

Kurita on the *Yamato* soon got a message from Ozawa's strike force saying he was under continuous attack by enemy aircraft and wanted to know the conditions around the main fleet, since he was approaching it. According to the battle plans, the Japanese Air Force was supposed to give the fleet full support during the fighting, but not one Japanese aircraft had yet shown up overhead. Kurita was at a loss as to what to do next. He suspected the worst of the air strikes was yet to come.

* * *

Thirty minutes later another formation of enemy planes appeared on the horizon. They closed in fast, dropping their torpedoes from a great height. The weapons fell spiraling to the sea, carving the water's surface with a great net of crisscrossing trails. Most headed for the *Musashi*.

"Full turn to starboard! Reverse direction hard aport!" The chief navigator screamed frantically over the main deck speakers.

The ship lurched violently as three more torpedoes found their mark, two to port, one to starboard. Torrential waves from the explosions crashed over the main deck, sweeping a tide of blood and dismembered bodies before them.

"Can still travel at twenty-four knots," the *Musashi* signaled to the *Yamato* after the attack.

The fleet held its formation. The *Musashi* zigzagged in wide sweeps along with the other ships in the First Squadron. One-third of its machine gunners were dead or wounded, but the rest continued to concentrate fire overhead. Enemy aircraft dropped into the sea, but the Americans were relentless. The next attack struck the port and starboard sides, followed immediately by two more torpedoes to starboard. Seawater poured into the vessel's lower decks. Then a bomb made a direct hit in the bow area of the main deck, killing scores of doctors and wounded crewmen in the forward infirmary.

Torpedo damage was concentrated in the *Musashi*'s mid to fore sections, and the entire area under the fore section's mid-deck was flooded. The bow was at a ten degree list to starboard. The defense director activated the pumping system and supervised measures to prevent further flooding.

"Twenty-two knots possible," the *Musashi* reported, its speed only slightly hampered by the damage. It continued zigzagging along with the fleet. The enemy aircraft had gone.

"Gunners may leave their stations," sounded over the speakers, and the exhausted men dropped to their knees. The main deck was littered with gore, and the screaming of the wounded cut through the silence like a jagged blade.

The air ducts and hatches to the main deck had been shut during the attack. Hot exhaust fumes from the engines filled the ship's hull, making the heat on the lower decks almost unbearable. The able-bodied burst topside into the open air drenched in sweat.

The forward infirmary, where the surviving injured sat silently in shock, was awash with blood. The functioning areas of the ship's infirmaries could not handle the unrelenting flow of injured, and casualties overflowed into the nearby officers' quarters.

The *Musashi*'s damage control crew was unable to correct the battleship's forward list. A torpedo, entering through an opening made by a previous explosion, had penetrated the ship's underwater defenses. The list in the bow reduced the vessel's speed to sixteen knots, and it soon fell far behind the rest of the fleet.

The enemy realized that the loss of the *Musashi* would be a serious blow to the Japanese Navy, and the attack planes had concentrated their firepower on her alone, leaving the other vessels virtually unscathed. Now, like a great but mortally wounded beast, it struggled, trailing the fleet as it slowly disappeared over the horizon.

# 26
## The Sinking

The commanding officer of the No. 3 pumping room telephoned the bridge to report that the hatches to the room were jammed. The men inside the room did not know they were flooded in. He had noticed that the *Musashi* was listing forward and asked how badly the ship had been damaged.

The bridge responded, "Everything is proceeding according to plan. We're still trying to blast through your hatch. Keep up the good work!"

The oxygen in the room began to thin and the temperature rose. The officer reported to the bridge as, one by one, his men collapsed. His own words grew shorter as he gasped for air. He never complained that he was in pain, but, finally, his voice too faded.

"Man battle stations!" the alarm rang again at 2:45 P.M.

Almost 100 enemy aircraft were heading directly for the *Musashi*, isolated on the ocean surface. Frustrated crewmen cursed the enemy's obsession with their crippled ship.

The *Musashi* continued to try to avoid enemy fire, but due to its enormous loss of speed, eleven torpedoes managed to hit both sides of the hull, ten bombs struck from above, and six bombs exploded close to the ship. Geysers of water rose over both sides. As the bombs exploded, smoke enveloped the deck to the point that the remaining crew could no longer see the enemy aircraft above them. More machine gunners were killed, and the crewmen of the *Maya* took their places. Most of the machine guns were overheated, however, and only a few could be fired.

166

One of the bombs hit the anti-aircraft control room over the No. 1 bridge. The bridge let out a huge roar as it collapsed like a demolished building. The explosion took the lives of the chief navigator and anti-aircraft commander, as well as five other senior officers. Captain Iguchi sustained serious injuries to his right shoulder.

With the loss of many of its major control rooms, the *Musashi* had finally sustained fatal damage. The ship was listing ten degrees to port, which was corrected to six degrees by the ship's pumping system, but the sagging at the bow had deteriorated from four meters to eight, and seawater was sweeping over the bow onto the main deck.

As the ship's speed fell to six knots, its machine guns were still firing at the enemy aircraft above. The captain went to the infirmary for medical attention, and the second in command, Lieutenant Commander Kenkichi Kato, took the helm. At this point Kurita sent the destroyers *Kiyoshimo* and *Shimakaze* to the *Musashi* to attempt to escort her back to San Jose.

After launching their entire cargo of torpedoes and bombs, the enemy planes circled above the fatally wounded *Musashi*, like vultures waiting for their prey to die.

The sixth attack had resulted in even more bloodshed. The severed heads and limbs of crewmen were scattered over the *Musashi*'s deck. The lights inside the ship had gone out, and even the backups were failing.

Kurita, seeing that the ship had suffered a fatal blow, ordered the *Shimakaze* to take off the surviving crew of the *Maya*. Captain Iguchi returned to the ship's No. 2 bridge with bandages wrapped around his shoulder and head and resumed command of the ship. The port-side list had grown worse.

The *Musashi* got its last signal from Kurita: "Proceed at best speed to a nearby island. Anchor inside the reef and land your crew and supplies."

Kurita realized that the fatally damaged *Musashi* could not make it back to San Jose.

Iguchi decided to anchor inside a reef along the northern coast of the Sibuyan Sea. He pointed the ship's bow in that direction but the water in the hull had already leaked into the engine rooms. The engines stopped halfway to the reef. With the loss of the engines, the emergency lights failed, and the hull fell into darkness.

Iguchi ordered his second in command to evacuate the crew to the main deck. Oil- and sweat-stained sailors emerged from various hatches. They hesitated for a moment when they saw the carnage above, and then, with pale faces, they emerged onto the blood-spattered deck. The crewmen in the ship's stern had mistaken the explosions of the torpedoes and bombs as fire from the ship's own guns —they had no idea how bad the damage was. Over 200 injured were carried from the rear hatches.

By this time the hull was listing at twelve degrees to port. Iguchi ordered the crew to continue working the ship's pumping mechanism to straighten it out. He was still hoping to have the accompanying destroyers tow the *Musashi* to the nearest reef.

After assembling the surviving crew on deck, Kato stood on top of the No. 1 gun turret and shouted, "It took months and years of labor and the best materials to build this unsinkable, indestructible battleship. As we pump water into the starboard side to correct the list, move as many heavy objects as you can from port to starboard. Move everything you possibly can!"

The crew swarmed to the port side of the ship. Even the wounded joined in, moving anything that was not bolted down to the starboard side. Some even pushed the dismembered bodies of dead crewmen to starboard. But the shift seemed to have no effect on the ship's list, which only continued to worsen.

Iguchi finally resigned himself to the fact that the *Musashi* would sink. He sent up a signal that the accompanying destroyers should first take the wounded on lifeboats, and then draw up next to the *Musashi* to take off the rest of the crew.

He received the "understood" signal from the destroyers, but neither vessel made any attempt to approach. An irritated Kato had one of his men send the signal again to make sure it was properly received. Once again he received a clear "understood" signal in response, but both ships simply circled the *Musashi* at a distance. Kato realized that they were afraid of getting caught in the wake of the *Musashi* as it sank.

The sun began to set. Captain Iguchi called together his second in command, the ship's defense director, the weapons officer, the communications officer, and the chief engineer, and thanked each of them for their efforts on the *Musashi*. He then handed Kato a small notebook and said, "Give this to the C-in-C of the Combined Fleet."

Iguchi pulled out a silver pencil and gave it to Kato, adding, "This is a keepsake of your time on the *Musashi*."

Kato and the other officers stared blankly at Iguchi's offerings. The captain was going to go down with his ship.

"Captain, please let me stay with you," Kato pleaded.

"No. The second in command must always survive to report to the C-in-C. I am ordering you to be responsible for the surviving crew and the families of those who have died." Iguchi said each word deliberately and with resolve, then he went into the captain's quarters on the No. 2 bridge and locked the door from the inside.

\* \* \*

It was almost sundown.

Kato walked to the aft of the main deck and ordered the crew to fall in. He then ordered them to lower the flag on the rear mast. The emperor's portrait was carried away on the shoulders of two warrant officers as a trumpet sounded the national anthem. The flag on the rear mast was lowered slowly and folded on the deck. An officer held it close to his body as he and the two warrant officers holding the emperor's portrait walked at attention to the ship's port side. All three jumped overboard with their mementos. The remaining crew took a roll call among their respective divisions. They stood in order on deck and waited for the next command. The list had reached thirty degrees.

Finally, Kato yelled, "Prepare to abandon ship!"

His face was painfully distorted. He was still obsessed with the idea that the *Musashi* would not, could not, sink. But if he was too late in ordering an evacuation, many valuable lives would be lost. Just as Kato yelled the evacuation order, a grating noise rose over the deck. The ship's list had deteriorated to a point where the objects the crew had shifted to the starboard side of the ship had begun to slide back to port. Men screamed as they were crushed.

"Every man for himself!" Kato yelled in panic.

The list increased rapidly. Crewmen started jumping off the deck at the stern, which was sticking up like a tower from the ocean surface. Before they reached the ocean surface far below, they were screaming in horror. Most of them hit the battleship's huge screws before they reached the water. Crewmen were running along the battleship, and several men who jumped off the sides were sucked into the huge holes made by the torpedoes.

The distance from the deck to the ocean surface was between forty and fifty meters. Several of the crewmen jumping off the ship attempted to slide down its sides to break the fall, but many were cut and injured by the jagged barnacles. Some of the younger seamen could not even swim, and though their superiors tried every means of coaxing them to leave the sinking ship, they could not bring themselves to leap into the water.

A long line formed along the edges of the deck of people waiting their turn to jump. The ship tilted suddenly, stirring up a large wave as the vast hull swung to port. The bow pointed down into the water, with the stern towering prominently above the rest of the ship. The crewmen still clinging to the wreck under the darkening skies of sunset were gradually moving further and further toward the stern as the bow plunged into the sea.

After the bow had sunk below the ocean surface, the ship's bridges were submerged, and only the stern remained above water.

Ten to twenty crewmen could be seen moving further and further to the stern as it sank, some of them holding on to the propellers. These figures, too, soon disappeared from the ocean surface.

## Location of the sinking of the *Musashi*

# 27
## Captain's Log

**October 24–25, 1944**


As the *Musashi* disappeared into the ocean to the sound of a deafening roar, it created a vast whirlpool and violent waves. The men swimming nearby were sucked under. They would periodically spring up above the surface, only to be sucked down after a few seconds.

Suddenly, a flash of brilliant red lit up the sea, and a tremendous underwater explosion came from the area where the *Musashi* had sunk. Bodies were flung into the air on a pillar of seawater.

The death toll was far greater than one would expect from the number that had managed to abandon ship. The sound of human voices could finally be heard over the darkened waters of the ocean, and the choppy seas where the *Musashi* had been swallowed up were finally beginning to settle. The crew had disposed of almost all the combustible materials on the ship before it set out on its mission, so the flotsam on the water was minimal.

Nevertheless, pieces of lumber, tatami mats from the *Musashi*'s judo gym, jerry cans, and kit bags floated to the surface, and the survivors grabbed on to them as lifepreservers. Groups of survivors began gathering. A blanket of oil about fifty centimeters thick had spread over the water, and the survivors' faces were blackened by the residue. Some got oil in their mouths and choked, while others spit out a strange white foam. The warm oil made many of the men sleepy, and the seamen had to slap one another to stay awake.

The sky was filled with stars, and a new moon began to rise over the horizon. The ocean surface seemed to brighten.

A group of 300 survivors had managed to form a ring. One man began to sing the national anthem, and the others took up the song. When the national anthem ended, another sailor began singing military songs, which were eventually followed by popular drinking songs.

After everyone had lost their ability to sing, an uneasy silence fell over the survivors. Several heads had disappeared. Others were clinging weakly to their pieces of flotsam, their heads hanging over their makeshift lifepreservers. After a time some of the men began clinging to others from lack of strength. Seawater would splash and foam as their hosts tried to shake them off. In desperation, some brought their would-be saviors down with them.

Many of the men took off their clothing as time passed. Only the men who were naked did not have to worry about someone clinging to them for support: The skin on their black oil-covered bodies was so slippery that anyone who attempted to hold on could not keep their grip for very long.

About three hours after the *Musashi* had sunk, someone yelled, "Destroyers!"

Two destroyers were approaching, and the men who no longer even had the energy to sing regained some of their hope.

"Everyone who can call out together," someone yelled.

The men shouted. Some broke off from the circle and began swimming toward the vessels. But probably because the destroyers feared an attack from enemy submarines, they did not stop.

The voices of the men weakened in despair.

A spear of light appeared on one of the destroyers and reached out across the ocean surface to where the men were floating. As the beam of light came to rest on the circle of men, some of them could faintly make out a cutter being lowered from the destroyer's side. The cutter approached but stopped short. The rescuers had seen how many survivors there were in the water, and they were afraid their small vessel would be capsized by the rush of men trying to be saved.

The survivors began swimming toward the destroyers, which moved toward them, lowering ropes and bamboo rods from their decks. The survivors grasped desperately for the lifelines, but many of them, coated with oil, could not get a grip. Some sank helplessly into the sea.

In order not to be moved by the current, the destroyers had to keep their screws rotating. These were fatal to many of the survivors. Some who finally managed to get close to the destroyers could not resist the force of the current toward the propellers and were sucked in.

The *Musashi*'s ordnance commander had been lifted by his men onto a tatami mat from the battleship's judo gym. They managed to float him close to the destroyer. He was an expert swimmer and still had enough energy to swim to gather up his men, but when the rescue operation was finally under way, he swam into the pitch-dark sea, toward the area where the *Musashi* had sunk, and never returned. It was his way of taking responsibility for the *Musashi*'s failure to ward off the enemy attack.

The survivors who managed to get on board the destroyers fell on top of one another in exhaustion. The rescuers washed the oil off their bodies with gasoline and gave them water, then carried them below like lifeless packages.

Lieutenant Commander Kato immediately went to the bridge and begged the captain to continue the search. Shining a searchlight when enemy submarines were in the area was extremely dangerous, however, and the search was called off at 11:00 P.M.

Kato had been told that six of the men who had made it to the deck of the destroyer had died shortly after. He had their bodies tied to practice ammunition shells and thrown overboard. When the burial was over, Kato went to a bed in the captain's quarters and pulled out the small notebook that Captain Iguchi had given him.

The notebook, which had been wrapped tightly in oiled paper, was not wet. Kato unwrapped the book and began to read.

174

On October 24 we were attacked by enemy aircraft. I greatly regret the loss of this ship, which was not only the hope of the Navy, but also the hope of the Japanese people. However, I am very pleased that almost no damage was sustained by the other vessels in the fleet in this battle. I somehow feel that, as the main target, the *Musashi* managed to save the fleet.

I truly regret that though the *Musashi* showed its full anti-aircraft capabilities during the battle, it did not perform up to par with the other ships in the fleet. I feel personal responsibility for this. We shot too haphazardly and thus failed to hit our targets.

Although I intend to fight this battle out to the end, it seems now that we have come to the end of the line. It is 1855. I would like to write down all my thoughts, but it is already dark. In the worst circumstances, we will be forced to remove the portrait of the Emperor, lower the flag, and abandon ship.

Nothing has been lost in my belief that this war must be won, and that our country should prosper eternally. Everyone, please fight to the last and ensure our final victory.

Many of our men were lost today, and may their heroic souls be consoled. Even though the sinking of the *Musashi* is a great loss for Japan, I am somewhat consoled by the fact that this battleship shot down some enemy aircraft.

I feel I am one of the luckiest men on earth for having the chance to serve as I did.

It is 1905. We have just received word from the engine room that the trapped men there are still in high spirits ....

After reading the captain's diary, Kato drifted off into a deep sleep.

175

# Epilogue

One thousand three hundred seventy-six of the original 2,399 crew of the *Musashi* were rescued by the destroyers *Kiyoshimo* and *Shimakaze*. Because their arrival in Manila would have been tantamount to an announcement that the *Musashi* had been sunk, the Navy decided instead to send them to the nearby Corregidor Island.

After the survivors landed on the island, they climbed barefoot up the stone streets of the old Spanish city to a makeshift barracks in the mountains. The Navy wanted to be rid of anyone who had been a crewman on the *Musashi*. The survivors were given the name the "Kato Regiment," after their surviving second in command.

Four hundred twenty survivors were put aboard the *Santosu-maru* on November 23 and sent to Manila. From there they shipped out for Taiwan, but along the way the *Santosu-maru* was sunk by American submarines. The *Musashi* survivors were cast adrift on the ocean for a second time, for nineteen hours. When they were finally rescued, fifty of their number had died. They were sent back to Japan, where they were forced to live in confinement on one of the islands in the Seto Inland Sea.

Another 200 survivors were put aboard a newly renovated aircraft carrier on December 6. This ship, too, was torpedoed by enemy submarines about fifty nautical miles southwest of Nomozaki. Altering its original course, the aircraft carrier docked at Sasebo on December 10. The *Musashi* crewmen, with no identification to any vessel in the fleet, were immediately sent to Kure, where they ended up in the barracks of the Kurihama Paratroop Regiment.

Almost half of the *Musashi* survivors were never allowed to leave the Philippines. One hundred forty-six of them were assigned to the defense of Manila. After U.S. troops had retaken the city on February 3, 1945, 117 of the original 146 were listed as killed or missing in action.

# Index

180

# Appendix

## Japanese Technical Drawings

Reproduced from *Design and Construction of the* Yamato *and* Musashi
(Tokyo: Haga Shoten, 1971) by kind permission of Mr. Kitaro Matsumoto

# General arrangement of *Yamato*-class battleships

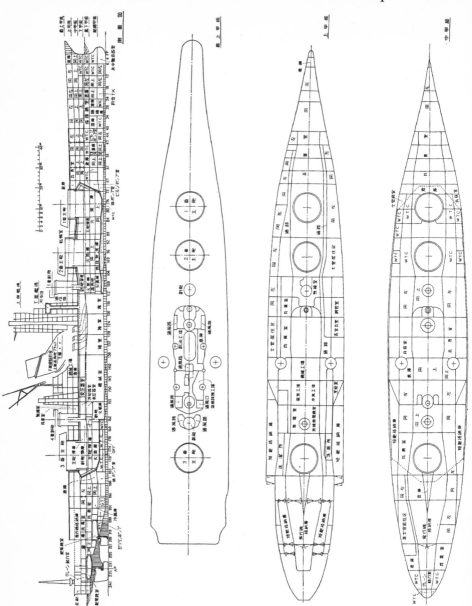

187

# Midship section of the *Musashi*

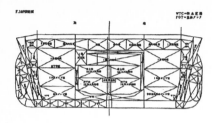

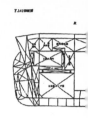

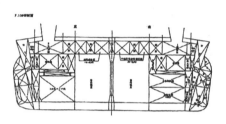

# Line and body plan of the *Yamato*

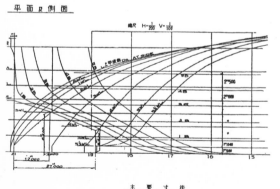

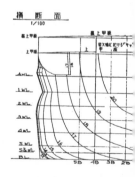

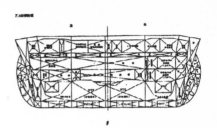

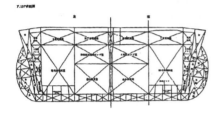

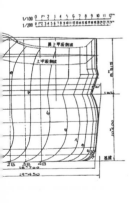

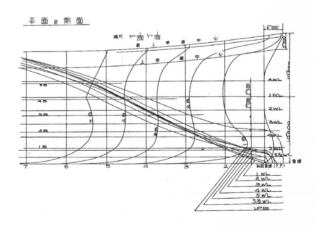

平面 及 側面

189

# Midship section of the *Yamato*

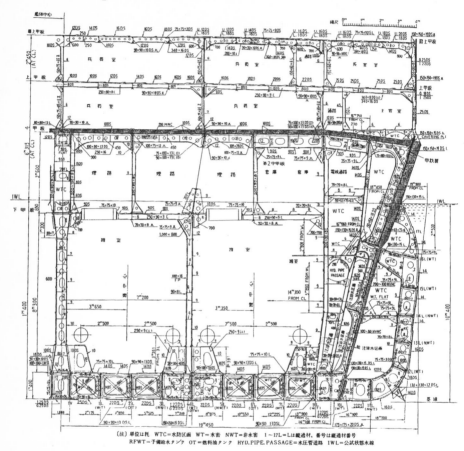

# Arrangement of protection

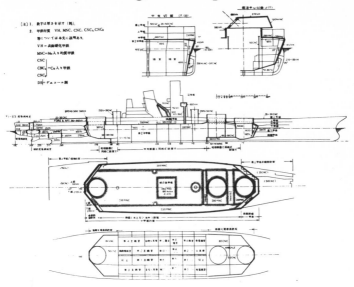

# Arrangement of deck armor plates

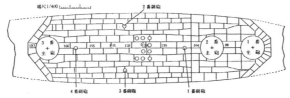

# Boat and plane stowage

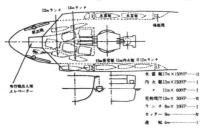

191

# Projectile stowage

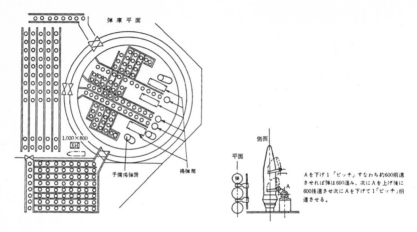

# Plan of galleys

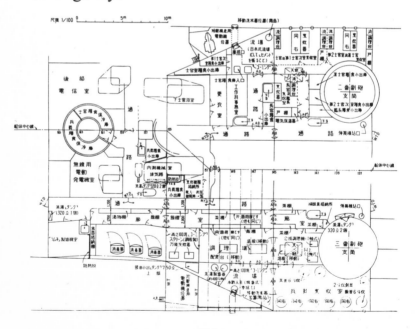

F96断面図

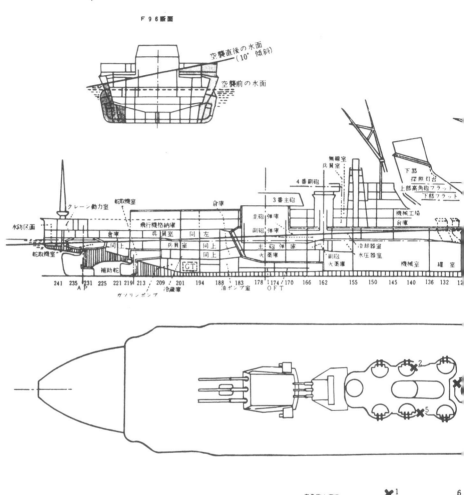

空襲直後の水面
（10°傾斜）

空襲前の水面

下部
探照灯台
上部高角砲フラット
下部フラット

無線室
兵員室

4番副砲

3番主砲

主砲弾庫
副砲弾庫

クレーン動力室
舵取機室

飛行機格納庫

食庫

機械工場
台庫

水防区画

食庫

兵員室

同左

主砲弾庫

冷却器室

舵取機室

同上

兵員室

同上

主砲
火薬庫

副砲
火薬庫

水圧器室

機械室

罐室

補助舵

同上

GT

241 235 231 225 221 219 213 209 201 194 188 183 178 174 170 166 162 155 150 145 140 136 132 12
A P
ガソリンポンプ
冷蔵庫
油ポンプ室
O F T

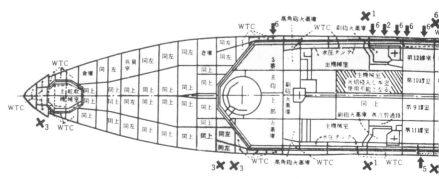

WTC
WTC
WTC
WTC

食庫
主舵取
機械室

同上
同左
同上

兵員室
同上

同上
同上
同上

同左
同上
同上

同左
同上
同上

同左
同上

食庫
同左

同左

同左

同左

高角砲火薬庫
WTC
WTC

副砲火薬庫
WTC

水圧タンク
主機械室

3番
主砲
上部
副砲
大薬庫
主砲
火薬庫

主機械室
火焔侵入し本室
使用不能となる

第12罐室

第10罐室

第9罐室

副砲火薬庫
蒸気管通路

主機械室
水圧タンク

第11罐室

WTC
WTC

高角砲火薬庫
WTC
WTC
WTC